The Meeting

AN AUSCHWITZ SURVIVOR
CONFRONTS AN SS PHYSICIAN

Edited by

BERNHARD FRANKFURTER

Translated from the German and annotated by

SUSAN E. CERNYAK-SPATZ

SYRACUSE UNIVERSITY PRESS

First Edition 2000
00 01 02 03 04 05 06   7 6 5 4 3 2 1

This work was first published in German in 1995 as *Die Begegnung: Auschwitz—Ein Opfer und ein Täter im Gespräch* by Verlag für Gesellschaftskritik Ges.m.b.H & Co.KG.

The paper used in this publication meets the minimum requirements of American National Standard for Information Sciences—Permanence of Paper for Printed Library Materials, ANSI Z39.48-1984. ∞™

Library of Congress Cataloging-in-Publication Data
Bewegnung. English.
    The meeting : an Auschwitz survivor confronts an SS physician /
  edited by Bernhard Frankfurter ; translated from the German and
  annotated by Susan E. Cernyak-Spatz.
      p. cm. — (Religion, theology, and the Holocaust)
    Includes index.
    ISBN 0-8156-0604-4 (cloth : alk. paper)
    1. Auschwitz (Concentration camp) 2. World War, 1939–1945—
  Prisoners and prisons. 3. National socialism. 4. Ostermann,
  Dagmar, 1920– Interviews. 5. Münch, Hans Wilhelm, 1911–
  Interviews. 6. Interviews—Austria. I. Frankfurter, Bernhard,
  1946– . II. Cernyak-Spatz, Susan E., 1922– III. Title.
  IV. Series.
  D805.5.A96B4913   1999
  940.53'094386—dc21   99-36798

To the memory of

BERNHARD FRANKFURTER

1946–1999

Bernhard Frankfurter was an international film director whose documentary film credits include *Capitalism in Thirds* (1975), *On the Road to Hollywood* (1982), *SS Nr. . . . Terminal Auschwitz* (1984), and *Love Life—Live Death* (1989). Before his death in 1999, he was also active as an editor, columnist, and scriptwriter, and he founded the Eastern-Western Media Network in 1994.

Susan E. Cernyak-Spatz is professor emerita of the Department of Foreign Languages at the University of North Carolina at Charlotte. She is the author of numerous articles and books, including *German Holocaust Literature* and *Hitler's Gift to the Jews: Translation of Norbert Troller Diaries.*

Contents

Preface

The injuries to my spirit and soul were harder to bear than the physical ordeal.—DAGMAR OSTERMANN

Having belonged to a criminal organization, whether voluntary or involuntary, does not necessarily make a man a priori a criminal.—DR. HANS WILHELM MÜNCH

In 1979, during my research of the extermination camp Auschwitz and the members of the SS stationed there, I examined the files of the 1947 war crimes trial of Cracow. The accused in this trial were SS members in leading positions at Auschwitz.

I became especially interested in an SS physician, the only one to be acquitted in the proceedings: Dr. Hans Wilhelm Münch. Hans Wilhelm Münch was head of the Waffen–SS Hygiene Institut in the extermination camp and had control over hundreds of male and female prisoners.

The reason for his acquittal was the fact that he refused to participate in selections, the activity that decided on the prisoners' life or death, as well as statements given by Polish prisoners about his actual assistance to the prisoners. But this physician was nevertheless a convinced National Socialist and an effective part of the extermination apparatus. The Hygiene Institute was located in Rajsko, a part of the enormous Auschwitz Complex. It was an integral part of the extermination industry of Auschwitz and—as strange as this might sound—an enterprise of protection. Its main charge was the protection of the SS forces from the threatening epidemics. The prisoners of course existed under catastrophic hygienic conditions.

It was considered a "normal operation" to "clean out" a barrack or block if typhus had broken out in the barrack. The inmates were gassed and the barrack was "cleaned" with the same gas, Zyklon B. The only difference between the two gasses was that the gas used for cleaning the barrack had a chemical marker warning of poison. The Institute, of course, also undertook "research." The beef, being supplied for bacterial cultures, was eaten by the SS, and human flesh of deceased prisoners was substituted for the cultures. I met Hans Wilhelm Münch for the first time in 1981 in Munich. He was at the time a country doctor in the Allgäu (an area in Southern Bavaria). The result of this strange encounter was a film of 80 minutes length, produced, written, and directed by me. The title is *SS Nr. . . . Terminal Auschwitz*. I interviewed Dr. Münch myself in this film.

Being aware of the janus-faced characteristics of a perpetrator who might have to some extent refused service to the Nazi machinery, I decided to make a second film in which this physician would be confronted by a female Auschwitz victim.

In April 1988, Dagmar Ostermann and the former Auschwitz physician, Dr. Münch, confronted each other for three days in front of three cameras. Today Dagmar lives in Vienna. She had been imprisoned in Auschwitz as "Geltungsjüdin" (term for a Jewish woman with one Christian parent under the Third Reich law) and survived by fortuitous circumstances. Her family background, owing to her Aryan mother, was of course rather mixed. Two of her uncles on her mother's side were National Socialists. The one living in Vienna had already been an illegal Nazi party member before 1938. I decided on Dagmar Ostermann for the filmed confrontation for two main reasons: her biographical background and her commitment to Holocaust commemoration. She visits schools throughout Austria as one of the "Zeitzeugen" (historical witness program in Austria that utilizes survivors and resisters of the Nazi period to give oral information to students). I have, however, also spoken to other Jewish women survivors of Auschwitz. Those talks have been incorporated in the essay.

Dagmar Ostermann and Hans Wilhelm Münch were not accquainted with each other up to the time of the production. We had agreed that before and during the filming of this confrontation the two participants would not have any private conversations between them. I did, however, talk with both participants beforehand about topics and questions without giving any interfering directions.

A film of the conversation between Münch and Ostermann has in the meantime been made available. The following text is a transcript of the film's dialogue. Ms. Karin Jahn has merely edited the dialogue somewhat. Only phonetic faults and repetitions were edited out. In 1994 an additional conversation with Hans Wilhelm Münch took place for the express purpose of inclusion in this publication; an additional conversation was taped with Ms. Ostermann as well. Since Karin Jahn collaborated in these additional interview sessions, she is listed in the text as participant in the conversations. My last meeting with Hans Wilhelm Münch took place in Auschwitz-Birkenau in spring 1995. For the very first time after being stationed there, the former SS physician visited the camp. He was accompanied by a female survivor who had been one of Mengele's "guinea pigs" as a child. Münch had been on fairly close talking terms with Mengele in his Auschwitz time. This last meeting was a rather strange event about which I will mention more in the essay.

The essay represents a journey into the innermost recesses of this historical topic, which today is as current as ever. Not the solutions to the questions, but the questions themselves form the main body of this text.

The dramatic structure of the text follows the actual events chronologically. The first part contains the transcripts of the film's dialogue. The second part consists of the follow-up conversations recorded by Karin Jahn and myself with the participants in Munich and Vienna, respectively. The appendix contains short biographies of Ostermann and Münch, a facsimile excerpt of the Cracow trial decision, and a map of the Auschwitz Concentration Camp.

The origin of the two films and this text reflect my preoccupation with what I call the "Minuskomplex Vernichtung" (zero-sum complex of Destruction; this concept is elaborated in the essay of the same title, which concludes this book).

To find a publisher for this text was a difficult undertaking. Contrary to assurances, lipservice, and the officially regulated manner of remembrance, there is little demand for internalizing one's own—as well as the common—history of our nation. It should be noted that this fact applies specifically to official institutions; it seems to represent the face of official Austria. But there are other faces who dare to look into the mirror of the past. To them I dedicate this book.

Vienna   Bernhard Frankfurter
Summer 1995

Introduction

It has been fifty-five years since I first met Dagmar Ostermann. Dagmar, then Dagmar Bock, was one of the inmate secretaries in the Political Section of the Concentration Camp Auschwitz. The date was February 1943 and I had just had the incredible fortune to be assigned to the Political Section Secretarial Commando. I had only barely arrived as a deportee from Theresienstadt to Birkenau, the extermination camp. I had gone through the customary selection at the ramp, had been sent to the group designated to live and had been processed into the camp, with its adjunct dehumanization of being shorn, tattooed, and clothed in the summer uniforms of dead Russian prisoners. We sixty-two women who had survived the selection from my transport were housed in one of the so-called quarantine blocks. Sheer ignorance of what could have been a direct trip to the death block, block #25, prompted me to approach the SS man standing at the side of the column when we marched out to work and offer my services as typist and secretary. I had been a secretary in Theresienstadt, and I thought the rules of applying for work would apply here as they did there. Fortunately the SS man, who happened to be the labor control officer, had a sense of humor considering my inappropriate behavior. He took my number, the only identity I possessed in that dehumanized society, and I was eventually sent to work in what was probably the most elite commando in the women's work force, the Political Section secretaries.

Dagmar, a member of that commando, was the first person who welcomed me with a hug as a fellow Viennese and became sort of my protector. She had been there since 1942 and knew the ropes. Unfortunately, my stay there did not last long. A letter smuggled by one of the prisoners to a man produced the standard punishment: the culprit as well as the newest addition to the commando were sent to Birkenau. Two Belgian sisters and I were the chosen victims.

We were shipped back to Birkenau to the outside commandos and almost certain death, either from starvation or disease.

Thanks to the unwritten laws of the women's camp in Birkenau that one has to help any woman who might have known you in the free world, or who might be from the same neighborhood, or even the same town as you were, I was saved from the outside commando by a longtime Slovakian inmate (spring 1942) and so began my administrative career in Birkenau. This fortuitous coincidence probably saved my life since another sort of unwritten rule was that if you once were in an administrative job in Birkenau, you could not be sent back to the outside commando and certain death.

Working in several office jobs in Birkenau, I ran into Dagmar again in 1944. She had been apprehended writing to her mother through an intermediary and had been sent to the penal commando, but again the unwritten rules prevailed. Being a prisoner of such long standing as she was, since 1942 (the officially calculated period of survival in an outside commando in Birkenau was three and a half months maximum), she knew enough Kapos and even SS Matrons to be given lenient treatment in the penal commando. (She also knew enough people in the kitchens and among the various block secretaries to always manage to find some extra food.)

In 1945, probably on April 29 or 30, on the deportation march from Ravensbrück, we stopped one night in the Ravensbrück satellite camp Malchow, in North-East Germany, and there was my Dagmar again. One would think that after both of us had survived and had found each other once more we would have stayed in touch. But at that point in time no one knew whether we would find anyone of our families alive and where we would be going.

I became a war-bride, moved to America, and as nobody here even wanted to hear about the Holocaust and my life during that period, I never talked about it. Unlike now when there is great interest in the subject, America lived for the euphoric post-war era and people like me were not allowed to disturb that state of well-being with our morbid tales.

The next time I heard from Dagmar was again an incredible fluke. My cousin Kitty, who had survived the war in Rumania and lived in Italy, met a young woman during a vacation at an Austrian lake resort. The young woman had a tattoo on her arm and Kitty mentioned that she had a cousin living in America who also had such a tattoo. One word led to another and soon I received a letter from Kitty telling me that Dagmar was alive and doing very well in Vienna. We started a correspondence and sent each other pictures of our children. The correspondence died down owing to the fact that our lives had taken such totally divergent directions. We had nothing to say to each other. Neither she nor I during that time ever mentioned Auschwitz-Birkenau.

Fast forward to 1972. I had finished my doctorate in Germanistics, had taken a job in Charlotte, North Carolina, and could finally realize my great desire, a trip to Europe. When I was in Vienna staying at my aunt's house, I searched the telephone book for Dagmar Ostermann, her married name. I found her. She was a successful businesswoman, as energetic and competent as ever. We reminisced a bit about camp, but mostly about our lives after camp. On consecutive visits to Vienna I always saw Dagmar. But not until she retired from her last business venture in the 1980s did she begin thinking about what now has become her lifework: Teaching the next generations not to forget the horrors of the Holocaust.

I had in the meantime developed a course on Holocaust studies at the University of North Carolina at Charlotte, and was also lecturing frequently at High schools and other Universities in North Carolina as well as in other States. Now our interests have converged, and I am proud to know that Dagmar has been honored by the Austrian Government with the highest medal of merit for her work. The Austrian Government has developed a program of what they call "Zeitzeugen," witnesses for the past, of which she is the absolute star.

When I was in Vienna last year she handed me a book that had been published by the documentary film maker Bernhard Frankfurter, called *Die Begegnung* (The Encounter). The book consists of a lengthy interview between Dagmar Bock-Ostermann and Dr. Wilhelm Münch, a former SS physician in Birkenau who had worked with the Hygiene-Institute in Rajsko, a section of the camp. My first reaction after reading the slim volume was: "This would be perfect for a text for my Holocaust course." There are many books written by survivors, a number of books written by perpetrators, many books written by researchers about the Holocaust from all possible aspects. But to my knowledge their is not one book pairing a survivor with a perpetrator in unrehearsed, spontaneous conversation.

In the dialogue Dagmar displays an uncanny ability to direct the conversation in the direction she decides. Dr. Münch is clearly on the defensive. He tries avidly to avoid making any remark that might designate him as a voluntary party member. He gives us a revealing insight into the mentality of a reluctant opportunist who tries to mitigate his decision to accept posting "to the South East," which, in spite of his denials, he must have known to be Auschwitz. Dagmar keeps leading him with her questions, prompting him to reveal more of his mentality than he would expose in an interview with an uninvolved reporter. "You were not a human being, you know that don't you," he says "you were a number, no more." In spite of his claims to the contrary he obviously followed the SS thinking. He even describes Dr. Mengele as a rationally thinking, objective scientist, and thinks nothing of it when Mengele coolly states that when he was through with experimenting on the twins they would go to the gas like all the others. His rationale for explaining why the starved, numbed prisoner can cope with the camp better than the newly arrived, healthy person is almost obscene in the convoluted way of his rationalization.

The reader has the feeling that over the years Münch built up all the defenses he quotes to placate his conscience so he could live with himself. He keeps repeating how he saved several women in his commando by subjecting them to useless tests, or how friendly he was with the men in his commando. As a prisoner of several years in Auschwitz, I can tell him that any SS man who stayed with a specific commando for any length of time would also become almost humane. Dagmar tells of that fact as well. It is sad to see that this man, who seems to have had almost humane instincts, managed to bury these instincts and shreds of decency under the rationale of expediency. Even in 1994, the year of the interview with Bernhard Frankfurter, he refused to accept the truth about his colleague, Mengele. Now as then, he uses the same justifications for his loyalty to his fellow physician. His justifications, for what he calls "passively" accepting the Nazi theories and the rationalizations offered for the murder of Jews and Gypsies, are a revealing insight into the mind of an inherently normal intellect who tries to justify his opportunism in the Holocaust period with the excuse of "coercion," which according to him he tried to mitigate with individual kindnesses to those under his command. However, his contradictory opinions and explanations about many of the atrocities he witnessed willingly make him appear a somewhat unregenerated fellow-traveler, then and now.

The most interesting factor of Dr. Münch's words is his attitude that he himself is a quasi-victim, that all he did was done under duress of the time and the circumstances. Bernhard Frankfurter in his thoughts about what he calls the Zero-sum complex, elucidates this fact clearly. It would seem that this has been a frequent form of testimony by perpetrators. We find similar expressions of "victimhood" of the perpetrator, for instance, in Peter Weiss's work *The Investigation.*

Dagmar Ostermann presses Dr. Münch hard for expressions of his reasons for not taking the many opportunities he had, and he did have them, for leaving the hell of Birkenau, in spite of the fact that he claimed to have suffered in and despised the service. She also reveals her past with great candor and detail. She does not hide the fact that in Birkenau one could survive if one reached the right position and had the right connections. She also shows the reader the unbelievable determination of women to survive if at all possible. Walking five miles daily back and forth with typhoid fever is no small feat. I should know; I survived typhus on the outside commando while removing rubble from bombed-out buildings and building roads.

Dagmar also gives the reader an insight into the deceptive practices of the Nazi regime vis-à-vis the Jews, such as the deportation of her father, after Jewish veterans of WW I like him had been promised protection from deportation out of Vienna and, subsequently, from Theresienstadt when they were sent there, as well as her own deportation to Ravensbrück and Auschwitz after her uncle had been promised her freedom by his fellow party members. We all know of the Nazis' superb ability at deception on a large scale, like Munich or Theresienstadt. But the individual suffering caused by such false promises brings the fact home all the more.

I knew when I read the book that there was a definite place for it in the body of Holocaust literature in America. I have tried to interfere as little as possible with the flow of the language. After all this is not fiction that one might change the wording, but the words of an actual conversation, one that needs to be preserved as closely as possible.

I have added a glossary as well as a register of names to the volume to allow the American reader to understand the rank designation and the special expressions of the camp jargon, as well as some typically Austrian usages.

Dagmar and I are engaged in the same enterprise, "Never to Forget." We must teach the next generations that, to quote Primo Levi, "If we forget the Holocaust, it can happen again, and next time it does not have to be the Jews."

Thank you Dagmar, for allowing me to bring your story and your remarkable skill as an interviewer to the United States. And all my thanks to Dr. Alan Berger for having the faith to persuade Syracuse University Press to publish it. My sincere thanks also to Mr. Bernhard Frankfurter and the Döcker Publishing House for authorizing the translation.

Neither Dagmar nor I have written any lengthy autobiographies that gather dust on the shelves of numerous libraries. Our work is in the tradition of oral history. The sight and sound of survivors recreating their experiences before youngsters, who will carry the memories to the next generations, has had an impact hundreds of such young people. May we be granted many more years to carry on our work, never to forget.

The Meeting

The Meeting

WE TALK ABOUT AUSCHWITZ:

VICTIM TO PERPETRATOR — PERSON TO PERSON.

IN THE BEGINNING

OSTERMANN: I am sure that you know my name: I am Dagmar Ostermann. You can rest assured that I did not make the decision to meet you lightly, but I did decide to do it. Somehow I seem to always have had an idea that, provided I survived the camp, I would one day confront one of my tormentors from that past. I am well aware of the extent of your activities but know nothing about your private life. One point would be of foremost interest to me: how did you link up with national socialism, and what fascinated you so much about the movement?

MÜNCH: Well, where do I start? To begin with I have to say one thing: as I see it, there is basically always some inhibition involved when I speak with a Jewish person, believe me. Your attitude, as you . . .

OSTERMANN: I have absolutely no inhibitions about talking to you . . .

MÜNCH: I always have inhibitions . . .

OSTERMANN: I have also no prejudices, and I want to stress that I do not hate. It is rather significant, that you claim to feel so inhibited about talking to Jews . . .

MÜNCH: Always . . .

OSTERMANN: Why do you feel such inhibitions?

MÜNCH: That is exactly what I must explain to you. You say that you know my personal history. Then you must be aware that I was acquitted with much fanfare in the second war-crimes trial ever held.

OSTERMANN: De jure, de jure.

MÜNCH: Yes, de jure. But in the head of every Jewish, former Auschwitz inmate a warning bell must go off that it simply can't be. That there is no such thing as an SS officer who was there for any length of time who did not . . .

OSTERMANN: I have to correct you there. That statement about the Jew is not quite fitting. I am of "mixed race," as Mr. Hitler used to say.

MÜNCH: I used the wrong expression. Let us say in the head of a former Auschwitz inmate.

OSTERMANN: That is right. It is a totally mistaken assumption that an Auschwitz prisoner, even if he was a "political" or "asocial" prisoner, did not have the same view of the SS and the individual guards as did the Jewish prisoners. He might even feel stronger about them because most of the time the families of these prisoners were also involved in the punishment meted out to them. But every former prisoner, whether he was in Auschwitz or any other Nazi camp, is shocked when confronting a former guard, regardless. Being Jewish or of Jewish-mixed descent, or whether a communist, or whatever, that has nothing to do with it.

MÜNCH: I would say as a Jew one is considerably more involved, wouldn't you say?

OSTERMANN: Well yes, we are probably more sensitized. That is logical. But I don't want to interrupt you any more . . .

MÜNCH: These are preconditions, so to speak, which simply exist. I just want to state on principle—there are always certain inhibitions. Just as you state that you have to brace yourself to talk to a former guard, so do I feel inhibited when I talk to a Jew. Because from my point of view he must think when looking at me: "He has been acquitted de jure, but it is simply impossible that there is not something rotten in his past."

OSTERMANN: That is precisely what interests me most in your past history. What could compel a human being of a certain intellect and with an academic degree to serve this regime, and, what's more, to serve it wholeheartedly to the bitter end? What fascinated him in this party to such a degree, that is what I would like to know. You do not have to go all the way back to the beginning of your life history. I'll be satisfied with a few guideposts to your past and your road to national socialism.

MÜNCH: As far as that is concerned I will have to disappoint you, because I have never been an ardent, convinced national socialist. That is also mentioned in my acquittal. And what's more, I came to the SS and Auschwitz through a very stupid coincidence. I have no national socialist past, none at all until the war.

OSTERMANN: You were never a party member?

MÜNCH: Of course I had to join the party in 1937 and I believe that . . .

OSTERMANN [interrupts] What was your reason for that?

MÜNCH: Very simply, as a hospital intern I would have never found a job in Munich.

OSTERMANN: There I have to contradict you. I knew many a doctor who was not in the party . . .

MÜNCH: That varied with the regional area. In Munich, the birthplace of the movement, I can assure you it was impossible.

OSTERMANN: You could have gone somewhere else . . .

MÜNCH: It was not even very difficult to do it . . .

OSTERMANN: That's just it. You just took the path of least resistance.

MÜNCH: Let's say I had no particular reason . . .

OSTERMANN: You simply took the easy way out . . .

MÜNCH: No. In 1937 I had no reason to be very strongly anti-Nazi. None of my relatives or close friends were ever persecuted. You could really not protest against anything, such as what was happening economically, for example. On the contrary, we could see that many intellectuals who had been in bad shape before that time saw their lot improve considerably under Hitler . . .

OSTERMANN: Of course, but you knew very well how it came to be that unemployment was suddenly ended, how certain intellectuals suddenly got their chance.

MÜNCH: That was not necessarily so . . .

OSTERMANN: There had to be some reason. The program was well known wasn't it?

MÜNCH: It was known.

OSTERMANN: The goals of national socialism . . .

MÜNCH: Right.

OSTERMANN: There were anti-Nazis, who did not have a single Jewish relative, who rejected the directions and goals of national socialism out of their own sense of decency, and they even fought the Nazis and put themselves in jeopardy. You can't make it that easy for yourself.

MÜNCH: Of course not, but it wasn't quite as simple as you state it either. You are looking at this from your point of view. Don't forget, how was that slogan? "The Jews are our undoing," wasn't it, that was the standard phrase.

OSTERMANN: I was a very young girl at that time; I really did not pay much attention to these things, but I must tell you honestly, even if I would never have been involved as I was, I would have never been attracted by that program.

From your point of view, you will say, that is easily said, because I was involved, but let me explain something to you. My mother is German, from a very religious Baptist family, and those are the sects that were particularly . . .

MÜNCH: I know them well . . .

OSTERMANN: [continues] strong Christians. My mother came to Austria as a very young woman, as a Red Cross nurse—I can show you a photo of her if you like—and became acquainted with my father. He was a first lieutenant in World War I, i.e., he had done his duty for the fatherland on the side of the Germans, volunteered twice for the front; I can show you a picture of him. That too belongs to our topic, because Hitler had said veterans who had fought for the fatherland of course would . . .

MÜNCH: . . . and so on [he knows the story of the promises] . . .

OSTERMANN: . . . be exempt and would not be deported. So, then my mother married that Jewish man. Neither the parents of her intended nor her parents were especially delighted about it, but the young people had their way, and I was the fruit of this union. My two uncles, on my mother's side, came to visit the Jewish brother-in-law in the beginning of the twenties—and this already shows their rather weak character— though being guests at the house of the Jewish brother-in-law, they joined the national socialist party and became so-called illegals. [In Austria partymembers remained illegals until 1938, but in the 20s even in Germany proper they were illegals]. You can see that my family was not quite average. As an adolescent I got an inkling of what the goals of the Nazis were, because I often visited my grandmother in Dresden. I went there even when Austrians were not supposed to travel to Germany. Thanks to a telegram from my grandmother, I received permission to visit her. That is how I got to know national socialism in its full flavor. Already at that time I had discussions with my uncles about the why and wherefore. Since half of my family were Jews and the other half Nazis, I could not expect a normal Jewish future. My uncles could not explain their fascination with Nazism to me; I got that later. Now can you tell me, from your present view-point, what fascinated you in that regime to the point of serving it as faithfully as you did?

MÜNCH: For a start, I have to say that there was nothing that fascinated me in that movement; I tolerated it. I tolerated it very rationally, and against all arguments from my family. One may call my mother an absolute, fanatical anti-Nazi. My father was rather disoriented. He was a scientist who had little interest in matters of politics or in life in general.

OSTERMANN: Your mother was never nationalistically oriented?

MÜNCH: Never! That is, she was nationalistically oriented, quite a bit even, but never national-socialistic. She hated that man Hitler with an un-bridled passion. And her arguments against the whole thing were to-tally irrelevant and therefore did not carry any weight with me. On the contrary, one could say that she pushed me . . . well, she could not pre-vent me from joining the party. I remember her saying, "But you are not really a convinced party member?" "Right," I said, "but I have no rea-son not to join the party and risk my entire career by not joining."

OSTERMANN: You could have chosen to move to another town.

MÜNCH: Changing to another town was not quite that simple. I only took my final exams in 1938.

OSTERMANN: You were not even finished with your medical studies in 1937 . . .

MÜNCH: No!

OSTERMANN: That meant you could not have continued your studies . . .

MÜNCH: I could have continued, but 1937 was the final date for joining the party . . .

OSTERMANN: And that date you did not want to miss, right?

MÜNCH: That's right. Let's put it another way. I ran out of arguments against joining. My main objection, or shall we say what I absolutely disliked, was the anti-Jewish policy of the party.

OSTERMANN: Shall we cut to the chase? What led you to Auschwitz?

MÜNCH: Normally only the carefully selected people of the old guard came to Auschwitz. I came to Auschwitz by a road that was anything but normal.

OSTERMANN: Is there such a thing as a normal road to Auschwitz?

MÜNCH: Certainly. The people of the first generation of concentration camp guards—all the commandants, and the wardens—all of them came there by the normal route, i.e., they received their training in Dachau . . .

OSTERMANN: They sure were the right ones for the job.

MÜNCH: They were a specifically groomed section in Himmler's realm. They were continually told that they were uniquely important and that their task would be uncommonly difficult, that they were distinctly different from all other people.

They were the ones who came to Auschwitz in what I call the normal way. I belong to the small group of the abnormal postings to Auschwitz. I told you that my family was absolutely against national socialism. I joined the party in 1937 because in order to advance in one's profession without special help, one had to belong. Anyway, in 1937 in Munich, still being a student, I would not have had the ghost of a chance to find a job as an assistant in a clinic or at the university.

OSTERMANN: Excuse me for interrupting you, but at that time [1937], you did not even have a chance yet to work in a hospital. You still were a student, weren't you?

MÜNCH: Yes.

OSTERMANN: And you did not even know at that time when you would finish your Abitur [equivalent of final high-school exams, but on approximately sophomore college level]. So how could you aspire to a position as assistant or anything like that?

MÜNCH: I was ready to take my state boards . . .

OSTERMANN: Were you such a good pupil that you advanced so rapidly?

MÜNCH: I was a miserable pupil, but a good student, [in high school European children are called pupils; in the university they are called students] . . . In that way I changed considerably.

OSTERMANN: May I ask what the topic of your dissertation was?

MÜNCH: My dissertation topic seemed strangely enough to fit perfectly into the Nazi period. It consisted of just a few lines, published in an important medical publication. There had been a competition dealing with bacteriological culture-media produced with Agar-Agar [a culture-medium containing agar, an extractive of red algae]. The aim was to find a substitute preparation that would not have to be imported.

OSTERMANN: And that was your total dissertation?

MÜNCH: No, to start with it was not even a dissertation, merely an entry in the competition. I had studied a bit of chemistry; I examined the problem, and I had an idea. I took the idea to the institute and told them that could be done such and such a way. The head of the institute—and this was probably symptomatic of the situation at the time in Germany—was a highly respected elderly counselor who had no love for the Nazis but who was quite glad that he had come across a young man who might represent a possibility for the counselor to make points with the Nazis. It had been the regime who had allowed him to participate in the competition; he therefore received me warmly. I made the experiments, and they worked.

OSTERMANN: And the dissertation, that still interests me . . .

MÜNCH: I wrote a temporary announcement to assure that I had the possibility to enlarge upon the experiment later and to prevent anyone else from taking it up. And there you have it. That announcement, consisting of a few lines describing the principal of my idea, I submitted as dissertation, and it was approved. That took care of the problem.

OSTERMANN: Isn't it rather significant that your doctoral dissertation has practically no medical value . . .

MÜNCH: Oh, but very much medicinal . . .

OSTERMANN: Probably partly medicinal, but you cannot claim that it had any medical value.

MÜNCH: But yes, the possibility of working in bacteriology was strongly connected to that culture medium. And that stuff was only available from abroad.

OSTERMANN: You really never thought of becoming a physician, isn't that so?

MÜNCH: Of course I did. I only wanted to show you with this bit of luck how little it took to become somehow involved with the Nazis, even if you had no particular liking for them. Look at it this way: what reason did I have as a totally average student, even before 1937, not to participate in a university sponsored competition?

OSTERMANN: You certainly did not pick a topic that a physician, who wants to be a healer, would normally choose, right?

MÜNCH: But look here, after that competition I wrote three or four purely medical papers before I was licensed. Some, of course, dealt with bacteriology because I worked afterwards at the institute during my practicum. As the practicum work did not occupy all my time, I continued working in research, and I only wanted to work in that direction. Things look different from today's viewpoint. Then every young doctor hustled to finish his military service before the final exam if possible, but at least immediately following it. Because after eight weeks of military service he would be an officer, a medical officer.

OSTERMANN: Well then, why did you not do that?

MÜNCH: Because that was just not my style. I was so opposed to militarism that I would never have thought to do something in that direction. I just put it off as best I could.

OSTERMANN: You were in the S.A.?

MÜNCH: No, no, never. I was . . .

OSTERMANN: You were *only* a party member?

MÜNCH: . . . just a minute. There was not a student in Munich who did not one way or the other belong to a so-called unit or formation. Not the regular SS, etc. But now we almost get into the Waldheim syndrome, whether he was really a member of the SS, because he was in their cavalry unit . . .

OSTERMANN: There is something else that I need to know. Now you so vehemently object to the military, but if you were in any political formation at all, these groups also used military training. Whether it was the SA or the SS, all of them had a military foundation.

MÜNCH: Any student at that time, who was not a gung-ho national socialist, would pick his university with a view to where he could get by with the least if he had to go into any military service.

OSTERMANN: What was the least for you?

MÜNCH: The NSKK, the national socialist motorized corps.

OSTERMANN: Isn't that a subdivision of the SA? My uncle, who was a fanatic motorcyclist, belonged to that unit.

MÜNCH: That's perfectly true.

OSTERMANN: But the NSKK was a purely political group with military structure. They certainly received a military training as well. There was discipline and drilling just like a military unit.

MÜNCH: You must allow me to correct you there. At the university things were different. The man in charge of these matters, not the NSKK, but the political training of the students, had to prove that every student in one way or the other was involved politically, that is, with the national socialists. And if the student changed schools at the end of the semester, he had to find out immediately at registration in which unit he would get politically involved. One always tried to find out which of the different units was the least bothersome. Sometimes it was simplest to join the SA, because there they just sat around, got their political training, lectures, etc., took their test and then they had done their duty.

OSTERMANN: So, according to you, no one could study at that time without being in the party or belonging to some political unit.

MÜNCH: One had to be in the NS Student Alliance, or, as in my case, in the NSKK.

OSTERMANN: Well all right, the NS Student Alliance is another matter altogether.

MÜNCH: No, no, that counted all right, but it was in Munich . . .

OSTERMANN: But it was not a military formation.

MÜNCH: That it was not, but it took much more time. In Munich, for instance, if you had a motorcycle, you were fortunate enough not to have to march on foot, but you took the bike to the roll call, made a few formation exercises, and went home on the bike.

OSTERMANN: But you were politically instructed. You knew what the Third Reich was all about?

MÜNCH: Of course.

OSTERMANN: You knew of their plans.

MÜNCH: No, no, no . . .

OSTERMANN: The things that were contemplated? You seem to avoid these questions assiduously.

MÜNCH: I am not doing that. As far as the Jews were concerned, everybody knew about the things Hitler had in mind with them. Everybody knew the Stürmer, everybody knew the rude and derogatory manner in which they talked about the Jewish question. Nobody can ever claim that they did not know that. But I can remember exactly what I thought about it at that time: "You can't take this sort of thing seriously." There were many others who thought like me at that time. That is cheap propaganda for the broad masses, that is like a soap opera, that was done because they needed a scapegoat for anything and everything that did not work right. The Jews were always good for that. Anti-Semitism has existed since ever and ever, only the tone is a bit different this time. We had always had Anti-Semitism, only now it is a matter of government propaganda, they really play it up . . . that is how we . . . how I saw it at that time.

OSTERMANN: I must interrupt you here. You cannot really call things like the bookburning in 1933 merely "playing it up." [Books of Jewish and so-called undesirable authors were officially burned in German cities in 1933].

MÜNCH: That's right . . .

OSTERMANN: Storewindows were smeared with paint, proclaiming loudly, "Don't buy at the Jews' stores." That was not the common customary anti-Semitism, the shall we say, folksy anti-Semitism; that was a higher form of that pattern. You cannot call this mere propaganda, if books are burned, stores scrawled on, and Jewish stores boycotted.

MÜNCH: That is what I meant to say. In my view the anti-Semitism was greatly hyped, to give it a broad appeal for the public. Because the little man—the average public—they were not anti-Semites; you know that. The actual anti-Semitism was more a matter for the intellectuals. The peasant in the countryside who dealt with the cattle dealer, who usually was Jewish, he was certainly no anti-Semite. That man Hitler simply had to exaggerate, we thought, his propaganda, his whole argumentation, how he screamed his speeches . . . All you had to do was to read that book of his [*Mein Kampf*] if you can stand to do that. Then you can see immediately where he comes from, all of us used to say. But then, whether you liked it or not, you had to add, "Maybe he is right!" Why? Because that appeals to the broad masses. Look at them! They are running to these mass meetings; no one forces them. And they don't march enthusiastically in the street because they get paid for it. No, no, it is Hitler's propaganda that is so effective, though it is directed at the lowest denominator, absolutely brutal and repulsive to an educated person.

OSTERMANN: Now you are contradicting yourself. You just said, that the worker, the farmer the lower classes were not anti-Semites, but on the other hand you claim Hitler was right because he certainly lured the people with his message. If none of the little people were anti-Semites, how could he lure them with his Jew baiting?

MÜNCH: I think you misunderstand me here. Look, anti-Semitism is based on the need for a scapegoat, isn't that so?

OSTERMANN: Of course.

MÜNCH: For centuries, that's clear . . .

OSTERMANN: There is something that I cannot agree on with you, since you talked about anti-Semitism among the intellectuals specifically. I simply cannot accept that among them anti-Semitism was worse.

MÜNCH: I can only tell you what I saw from my point of view.

OSTERMANN: After all, there were many intellectuals who did not have to leave Germany, being neither racially nor politically endangered. But they preferred emigration to remaining in a country were people

were attacked because of their religion or their nationality. By the way, at this point I would like to ask you something: What in your concept is a "Jew"? What does the word mean for you?

MÜNCH: That is a good question, but one that is difficult to answer from where I stand. Most of the Jews are not really Jews in the sense of being orthodox, observing Jews. I knew that from my schooldays ... When I lived in Dresden, I had several good Jewish friends in school. I knew the milieu.

OSTERMANN: We seem to talk past each other. What is "Jewish" to you? A race, a religion? Some kind of hard to define individual? What is a "Jew" for you? What do you understand by the word "Jew"?

MÜNCH: That is a difficult question to answer. I have had different views on that question during the different phases of my life. Again today I have a totally different view than I had then.

OSTERMANN: At that time, what was a Jew for you?

MÜNCH: My first impression of Jews I got in Dresden.

OSTERMANN: What was, or better, what is a Jew?

MÜNCH: The genus "Jew" does not exist, just as the genus "German" does not exist. My impressions during my schooldays in Dresden were thus: there were Jews coming out of the East after the war. Those were the Jews who were rejected by their own Jewish people in Dresden, because they behaved too, shall we say, fresh out of the ghetto. That was the one kind. And then we knew the other kind, the ones who had assimilated and had acquired a different mode of living. They were totally different from the ones who came into Germany in the 20's. That is why I already said that at that time, for me, there were two kinds of Jews. Only with those who had been in Germany for at least two generations, did I have any contact; most of them had been here even longer.

OSTERMANN: Hitler certainly did not make any difference between assimilated Jews and Eastern Jews.

MÜNCH: True, true . . .

OSTERMANN: Then you regard Jews more as a religious group, is that right?

MÜNCH: The Jews whom I was in touch with were not any more religious than myself.

OSTERMANN: Judaism in my view is neither a religion nor a nationality. Jews are a people, a people that has had different nationalities as well as different religions. But for Hitler, religion did not play a part at all. For him, Jews who had been baptized for generations were still Jews. So tell me, what made a Jew a Jew in the eyes of a German?

MÜNCH: During different phases of my life, I had different ideas about Jews and saw things differently, because one simply cannot put an overall label on what is a Jew.

OSTERMANN: But you can. It is a people with different nationalities and different religions determined by its surrounding, etc. But let us come to the point of our discussion. I am here as a Jew, as a half-Jew, or whatever you see me as, but I am here in the first place as a former Auschwitz prisoner.

MÜNCH: Correct.

ON THE ROAD THE SS AND AUSCHWITZ

OSTERMANN: That is why at this point I would like to learn how you came to Auschwitz and to the SS, respectively.

MÜNCH: Right. And that really was an unusual road. I stopped my narration at the point when I told you that I had not served in the military, and that represented a great advantage for me, because I could live as I chose. I cannot honestly say that I was a full-blooded pacifist, but I definitely had a tendency to pacifism, something that came from our family tradition. My maternal grandfather was in the Franco-Prussian War of 1870. The family came originally from the German-French border area. He had all kinds of difficulties in deciding where he belonged: was he French, was he German? Finally he decided to move to Switzerland . . .

OSTERMANN: O.K. So you were against the military.

MÜNCH: I was against the military, as far as I personally was concerned. But then, bang—there was a war on. I already was an intern at the time. And now all the younger medical personnel who already had done military service, all interns, were drafted immediately. And now the authorities were grateful for the few people who were not in the military, like me; they were important to assure the medical care of the civilian population. The very young ones, like me, were sent to the countryside to take care of country practices abandoned by their physicians (who had been drafted). That is how I found myself in the Bavarian Allgäu. Right at the beginning of the war, when everyone was anxious to settle his affairs before being drafted, I got married, because you did not know what might happen during a war. My wife was a colleague of mine in the same hospital.

OSTERMANN: Also a licensed physician?

MÜNCH: Yes.

OSTERMANN: She was a national socialist?

MÜNCH: My wife was quite happy with the arrangement; she could come with me. That worked out well. Both of us could work there, and we frankly had a wonderful time. Medically of course, it was a bit difficult to start with . . .

OSTERMANN: That was which year?

MÜNCH: That was late 1939, early 1940.

OSTERMANN: The war was already in full swing at that time, wasn't it?

MÜNCH: Right. With the war, all the troubles started. We just had barely time to get married, because when one was not on duty, the other was. Everything was a bit topsy-turvy, but we finally managed and were sent to the countryside, and as I said, medically speaking, it was difficult but very interesting work.

OSTERMANN: Dr. Münch, I don't like to interrupt you, but I am sure we can get back to this topic at a later time. I am right now interested in your past, and we are still in '39, '40, '41, and we have not arrived at your Auschwitz stay yet.

MÜNCH: That happened rather quickly.

OSTERMANN: So you and your wife were country doctors during 1939 and early 1940. But how and when did you get to the SS and how did you land in Auschwitz?

MÜNCH: That's right. That happened in an unusual way. There we were in the country making a comfortable living, during '40 and '41. I did have to work hard. In the meantime, we also had a child. In one way, it was an ideal situation; on the other hand, there was plenty of stress. The stress was mostly emotional. I felt a bit guilty, seeing that I, as a young doctor, sat comfortably in the country whereas older colleagues, for whom I substituted, were on the front. One of them had already been killed, and there I sit in the country and have to listen to the wives of these colleagues telling me how their husbands went to the front with severe physical handicaps . . .

OSTERMANN: How come you did not volunteer? Doctors were needed.

MÜNCH: I did, I did. Already in 1941 I started to sign up. My wife was not exactly wild about that, you can imagine. But I really felt a severe inner conflict: to join or not to join.

After much soul-searching, I finally decided to enlist. That was rather difficult, because in our region, three different regional offices overlapped, and I had been declared UK [stands for "unabkömmlich" meaning "indispensable"]. The fourth authority was, of course, the medical board. That was the overriding authority, who had also declared me UK.

OSTERMANN: Don't you think your past connection to the NSKK played a part in your assignment [kept you out of the military]?

MÜNCH: Nobody cared about that. I even asked my sister...

OSTERMANN: Don't you think that that past kept you from the "Barras"? [Austrian slang for "military"]?

MÜNCH: I beg to differ. I asked my sister to see that I could be drafted. My sister, who had worked for an attorney before the war, now worked as secretary for the office of the general staff, and therefore knew all the really important people. She and they all tried to help me to enlist, but it was absolutely impossible. Believe me, I went from Pontius to Pilate to find a place that would accept my enlistment, but nothing worked. And one day, when I was again cooling my heels in some office in Munich, I ran into an old acquaintance, a former colleague with whom I had worked at the Hygiene Institute. His name was Strassburger. I did not know whether he was Jewish or not. In any case, there he was and looking prosperous. "How are you?" "what are you doing?" "I've got a nasty problem." And I told him my story. "Well," he says," I can manage that for you. All you have to do is enlist in the Waffen-SS." The Waffen-SS was being sold to prospective recruits as a legitimate part of the army, and I had already tried my luck there.

OSTERMANN: But you knew all about that SS Institution?

MÜNCH: You don't quite understand that. For the average John Doe who sat in the countryside as a physician, the SS was a purely military unit. I had tried to enlist there too, but it did not work either. So my friend said, "I'll get you into the Waffen-SS." And I said, "Fine, but how are you going to do that. What can you do?" "Well", he said, "I am now in Berlin and ..." He sort of dodged the issue. I go back home and after a relatively short time all the UK positions are open, and I am ordered to report to the Waffen-SS.

OSTERMANN: Which year was that?

MÜNCH: 1942

OSTERMANN: In the beginning or toward the end of '42?

MÜNCH: To finish off this part of the story... I'll never know how it was possible, how he managed it. Strassburger, he probably was a Jew, to judge by the name.

OSTERMANN: That does not mean anything. Rosenberg was also not a Jew and he had a Jewish name.

MÜNCH: Maybe he was not Jewish, fine. In any case, he was on Heydrich's staff.

OSTERMANN: Then he could certainly not have been a Jew.

MÜNCH: He could have been one, nevertheless. In my experience that was quite possible. I never met him again, but there are quite a few clues that Heydrich frequently used Jews to get into certain situations. I also heard, from another acquaintance, that Strassburger worked as a spy in Portugal.

OSTERMANN: That man Strassburger was also an SS member?

MÜNCH: All I know is that he was on Heydrich's staff.

OSTERMANN: To be in the SS you had to have proof of Aryan descent all the way back to the forefathers.

MÜNCH: Heydrich could do anything he wanted. Strassburger was a good friend of Heydrich's, from childhood and from school. I learned about that from the other acquaintance I mentioned.

OSTERMANN: To me that sounds like a lot of probabilities, not facts. What I want to hear now are facts.

MÜNCH: My whole road to Auschwitz was littered with a lot of such improbable events. Only life could create such coincidences.

OSTERMANN: So you joined the SS . . .

MÜNCH: Yes, well, I joined the SS and I got an abbreviated training that lasted only a few weeks.

OSTERMANN: And you had no special qualms about belonging to the SS?

MÜNCH: But I belonged to the Waffen-SS. You will have to take my word for it because I have no way of proving it, but I was totally convinced that it was a military unit.

OSTERMANN: You really thought joining that unit was going to get you directly to the front?

MÜNCH: Absolutely . . . directly to the front!

OSTERMANN: That was in what year?

MÜNCH: That was sometime in the winter of 1942–1943. So then we had to fill out a number of forms, previous education, training, what you did in your civilian life, etc. Well, I was a country doctor; plus, I had my bacteriological training at the Institute of Hygiene. That knowledge seemed to be very much in demand. The culture medium that I had developed was supposed to be tested under primitive conditions. Once I had been in Turkey on such a test, so to speak, under field-lab conditions.

OSTERMANN: That is where you got some experience, isn't it?

MÜNCH: Right, and because of that experience, I was assigned to the Waffen-SS Hygiene Institut.

OSTERMANN: Aha . . .

MÜNCH: That was the name: Waffen-SS Hygiene Institut with headquarters in Berlin.

OSTERMANN: I must interrupt you once more. It seems you again did not get what you actually aspired to: to be posted to the front.

MÜNCH: But of course I thought I did! The workplace of the hygiene medics were the field laboratories, the bacteriological examinations of the troops in the military hospitals, etc.

OSTERMANN: Aha, so you still believed that you were posted to the front?

MÜNCH: At least, let's say, to an important medical position in that whole operation. Because I really cannot claim to have volunteered for the real front. After all, I had to consider my children.

OSTERMANN: But that is what you wanted all along.

MÜNCH: . . . and my wife.

OSTERMANN: You wanted that to start with.

MÜNCH: I wanted to be drafted.

OSTERMANN: That is just it.

MÜNCH: We might as well call it that.

OSTERMANN: To be drafted and to go to the front, are those two different things?

MÜNCH: Certainly they are different. But if you voluntarily enlist, you normally are sent to the front. Anyone knows that.

OSTERMANN: Right.

MÜNCH: Well, then, that was my rationale. I was satisfied with this rationale, and my wife as well. I was sent to Breslau, to wait for assignment. There I did examinations of young recruits for the draft board, mostly coming from the Banat [part of Hungary] and other places, who had been drafted into the Waffen-SS. They were not volunteers, but draftees, because they were ethnic Germans. We all did our job there and were told that we would be assigned to our respective units eventually. I was sent to the Waffen-SS in Berlin, and in Berlin I was told I was being sent to . . . I forget what they called it . . . they did not call it field laboratory . . . you are sent to . . .

OSTERMANN: It does not have to be that precise.

MÜNCH: I remember. The unit was called South-East, South-East, that was it . . . And where was that? In Auschwitz.

OSTERMANN: And you did not become suspicious when you heard that?

MÜNCH: At that time I really did not know yet what Auschwitz was.

OSTERMANN: You mean to tell me that you had already been several weeks with the SS and had never heard any mention of Auschwitz?

MÜNCH:: Not a word, I can assure you.

OSTERMANN: And that in 1943?

MÜNCH: I can assure you that, even in 1944, I still met several members of the Waffen-SS, physicians in clinics, in field hospitals, who had been at the front already and who never had even heard of Auschwitz. Maybe they had heard a rumor about it. These people would ask me, "You are being sent to Auschwitz. What the devil is that?"

OSTERMANN: That does not seem believable, to be honest, because at that time, the knowledge of Auschwitz was fairly wide spread, and I would say the whole population knew of it already.

MÜNCH: That's right, right.

OSTERMANN: And even in the interior of the Reich, it was no secret.

MÜNCH: But in Breslau, for example, they did not know. There you could run around in the SS uniform and no one would connect that with Auschwitz. However, closer to Upper Silesia, when you got into the vicinity of Kattowitz, and you wore an SS-uniform, people would visibly shy away from you.

OSTERMANN: Ah yes. The Gestapo headquarters was located there.

MÜNCH: I myself did not notice it that much, but my wife certainly did; she could visit me in Breslau as long as we were not assigned yet.

OSTERMANN: And you took her right away along to Auschwitz?

MÜNCH: We tried to figure out what was the best way for my wife to get home from Breslau. We looked at the train schedule, and the best route was via Prague. "O.K.," I said, "then you can come along with me. Via Kattowitz you get to Prague and from there directly to Munich." But she noticed that people sort of moved away from me. I did not notice that. Well, so, I got to Auschwitz, and only then did I notice what was going on there.

OSTERMANN: And you did not take the initiative to say . . . "No way, I do not stay here!"

MÜNCH: No, of course not. And why? Because I knew that the Hygiene Institute, where I was posted, was outside of the camp. I am not sure you know where it was located.

OSTERMANN: I know, I know very well. It was approximately 1½ kilometers from the camp.

MÜNCH: Well, there I was, and the second guy who was lured into the SS by Strassburger like I was, Obersturmführer Weber, was my immediate superior. I knew him from Munich; he was a few semesters ahead of me at the university. Of course I asked him immediately, "Tell me, what is actually going on here?" Well, he told me everything right then and there, but he added, "We, however, have nothing whatsoever to do with that. You do your labwork here and nothing else, to start with. There'll be some added work later. I have been here now for more than a year and I never have had anything to do with that matter. No one has ever ordered me to make a selection or anything bacteriological in the camp directly. There is no future in asking for a transfer. You will never get out of here. The boss in Berlin will not transfer anyone who has been assigned here. There is a serious personnel shortage. Without Dr. Mrugowski saying you can get out, you won't get out. And let me advise you strongly against trying for a transfer."

OSTERMANN: Well, there I must contradict you again. Because I know of enough cases where people came to the SS, and they did not approve of what was going on there. The worst that could happen to them was that they were sent to the front. But there was no coercion to stay within the camp area.

MÜNCH: Do you really believe that we would be sitting here together or that I could have survived the war-crimes trial in Poland if there were no coercion?

OSTERMANN: Certainly.

MÜNCH: That is exactly what I want to explain to you at length.

OSTERMANN: I do have some information about Auschwitz, as you might assume. I don't know how well acquainted you are with Auschwitz's bureaucratic structure, but I worked in the Political Department [Gestapo section and prisoner administration of Auschwitz-Birkenau].

MÜNCH: But then you must know a lot . . .

OSTERMANN: And I also know a lot about what was possible and what was not. I was not so ignorant of the time and place that I don't know what the possibilities were. And, therefore, I know of the possibilities that the lowest SS man, as well as the higher ranks, had to refuse certain assignments, or to refuse to enter the camp area, period.

MÜNCH: But that is exactly what I did. May I continue? In the meantime, 6 months had passed. The prisoner commando in the lab consisted of approximately 100 people, 100 human beings. I can honestly say that with most of them, with at least half of them, I had a friendly relation . . . They were all physicians and people who, for the most part, had worked in labs or institutes.

OSTERMANN: The majority were Poles; there were some Jews among them.

MÜNCH: Only a few. Perhaps we had ten Poles; for the most part it was a Jewish commando. In the meantime I had become, for all practical purposes, the head of the lab. Because Weber was needed for other things, he had to be frequently in Berlin, in the Rhine area and the Ruhr area, where they were building the new underground facilities, where camps were supposed to be installed. So there I was, practically the head of the institute. And when I talked with the prisoners in the commando about what might be the best way to get out, to be transferred, they all begged me, as one, not to do that, because I had such potential to do something not merely for the people in the commando but for the camp inmates in general. All went well in this way until the Hungarian transports arrived. That was during the summer of '44. Then the order came: every physician has to go to the ramp and select. I also got the order to report to the ramp. I went immediately to the camp commandant and told him, "No way. I won't do that. Do what you want with me; I won't do it." The commandant did not accept that very well and sent me to his adjutant, who simply ordered me to the ramp the day after next. He'll be there, he says, and he will see to my initiation.

OSTERMANN: Yes . . . ?

MÜNCH: So I went to see Weber, who just happened to be in Auschwitz, and I said, "I won't do it. Now help me think what to do." And he said: "You go to Berlin and report to Mrugowski, the boss of the Hygiene Institute." That same night I went to Berlin, got to Mrugowski, and explained my situation to him, and he immediately started telephoning with the commandant. It seems the commandant wanted a favor from him also, and one hand washed the other. And so Mrugowski managed to have me exempt from ramp duty, from having to do selections.

OSTERMANN: Yes . . . ?

MÜNCH: Of course, the news of that exemption got around the camp very quickly. Many prisoners knew of it, and they worked all the harder to keep me from trying for a transfer from Auschwitz.

OSTERMANN: Another interruption, if I may. OK. You did not select at the ramp. You did not kill any Jews. But you worked in the vicinity of the area where all these crimes took place. You could do your scientific work with the smell of corpses permeating your nose. And your scientific labor served a regime that was dedicated to extermination. I am certain as a physician you have taken the hippocratic oath, and with this oath you affirmed that you wanted to help mankind, to heal the sick, but not to kill human beings. Even if you did not kill with your own hands, you expressed your agreement by being there and remaining there. I cannot imagine that one cannot break out of that orbit, with an honest effort. I remember an incident that I think you should hear.

There was a certain SS man named Böck. He drove the so-called Sanka [Sanitätskraftwagen (Ambulance)]. One day he was told to transport the Zyklon-B gas cans to the crematorium. He knew probably that Zyklon-B was a pesticide against lice, a pest that was very prevalent in the camp and resulted in typhus and spotted fever. However, when he saw what they used the Zyklon-B for, he refused to ferry the next transport of Zyklon-B to the gas chambers. He was neither shot, nor did anything else happen to him. He disappeared from the camp area and we found out that he had been sent to the front. There was also another SS man working in the Political Section, a certain Corporal Pyschny. He also was acquitted in the Polish war-crimes trial; he was from upper Silesia, near Cracow. That Pyschny was more often in the "Bunker" [Gestapo prison Block in Auschwitz I] than he was active as a guard, because he tried to stand up for the prisoners. That is why he was acquitted, especially on the recommendation of the Poles, with whom he had had special contact in camp. The mere fact that you knew of everything that went on and that you stayed there nevertheless, in spite of being a physician, a physician who had taken an oath to help mankind, that you could work in such a surrounding . . . I could well imagine, if you had said, "I cannot do any valid scientific work in this surrounding, it is impossible for me as a humanist and physician," that they would have assigned you to another area outside of the camp if your scientific contribution was valuable enough to them.

MÜNCH: I agree. But we spoke of extraordinary conditions and the situation continued to be extraordinary. By now it is clear that I came to Auschwitz in an unusual manner, that it was not the normal career progression.

OSTERMANN: True, that was not the normal path to Auschwitz.

MÜNCH: And now we have arrived at the point of explaining why I stayed there. First of all, the prisoners pleaded with me to stay. I was not involved in anything where I could possibly . . .

OSTERMANN: Where you would have gotten your hands dirty . . .

MÜNCH: . . . where I would have gotten my hands dirty. But . . .

OSTERMANN: But you were involved nevertheless!

MÜNCH: But something else happened at the time. There was in block 11, if you know what that was . . .

OSTERMANN: Oh yes, that was the execution block.

MÜNCH: No, I meant block 10, my mistake . . .

OSTERMANN: Block 11, that was the block with the Bunker.

MÜNCH: Yes, that one belonged to the Political Department. Block 10 was the block of . . . what was the name? Clauwith, Clauberg?

OSTERMANN: Clauberg.

MÜNCH: Yes, he had his experimental station there. In it there were about twenty to twenty-five young Jewish women. They remained there after Clauberg had already left. They were assigned to the Hygiene Institute because we needed, how should I say it, spit.

OSTERMANN: Saliva.

MÜNCH: We needed Saliva to determine bloodgroups. Well, these women were left behind, and now they were supposed to spit. We fed them well, so that they could spit well. All of a sudden we are told, "No more spit needed." And then they said, "Well, that takes care of your project. The women can be gassed." And I was supposed to take care of all that. Now came the dilemma for me: what do you do now? If you hand these women over to be gassed, you have as good as selected them yourself. After a sleepless night, my course of action was plain to me. We simply had to find more experiments for these women. It was rather difficult to persuade the local headquarters, because this was a project outside of the normal rules, but after much difficulty, I succeeded. So I went to the women and told them, "I can prevent your being returned to the camp. I have to do a few experiments with you, and those experiments will have to include a few shots, otherwise, I cannot justify them. You must tell everyone that these experiments are very painful and disagreeable, so that the headquarters people do not get wind of anything."

OSTERMANN: But you had to tell them at headquarters what these experiments were about, didn't you?

MÜNCH: We injected them with a serum. We dealt with granuloma of the teeth. You know what that is? [nodules of chronically inflamed tissue with granulation, in this case probably on the gums].

OSTERMANN: Yes, I know what that means.

MÜNCH: These granuloma develop from bacteria and partially through viruses. The viruses had been isolated, and a vaccine had been produced from them. You might not know that, that is a bit complicated . . .

OSTERMANN: Oh, but I know that also.

MÜNCH: OK. The vaccine had been produced, and it was being injected, and we would observe whether immunity could be attained through this vaccine. The experiment was really on the up and up. And with this experiment I could save the lives of these women.

OSTERMANN: But you must have been aware of the fact that you could only momentarily save them from the gas.

MÜNCH: No, that was just not the case, but . . .

OSTERMANN: Because you knew what the actual program was. That everyone, absolutely everyone, sooner or later, was destined for the gas; only the fast progress of the war allowed us to stay alive. Even the Political Department was going to be gassed, because we were so-called bearers of secrets.

MÜNCH: We had a really special plan for how to get them back into the camp one by one.

OSTERMANN: Oh, sure. But in the camp, it was also planned to gas everyone, Jews, Slavs, or Gypsies.

MÜNCH: But my dear woman, please try to understand! I had in the meantime established the best possible rapport with these people, after having spent so much time with them.

OSTERMANN: Certainly, but you must have known that this was just temporary . . .

MÜNCH: I kept asking myself, where in the sense of the Hippocratic oath can you be more effective at this point in time? You could try to report to the front, which you probably won't be able to do, because Mrugowski might let you out of Auschwitz, but never out of the SS. And so it became quite clear to me, that whether I was there or here, it did not make much difference. Above all, as long as one was in Auschwitz, it was quite possible that one might be assigned to a place where things were not done very humanely. Well, so I consulted with all those who were concerned with the situation, what I should do. And all of them, and I am not exaggerating, begged me on bent knees: "Please stay here and do as you planned." You should know better than anyone else that a drowning person grabs at any straw to survive. One never knows what life may bring. Things never work out as they were planned.

OSTERMANN: Another question!

MÜNCH: Just a minute! Please be good enough to let me finish.

OSTERMANN: Yes, all right.

MÜNCH: I saw my way clearly. I realized, that in this situation I could actually do a lot to help. You just mentioned before that the cadavererous smell permeated everything, that seeing all the horror was unavoidable. You know, when a human being is subjected to an extreme situation, even for a short time, you will find that he or she can not only get used to it, but can also cope with it much better than theoretically thought possible. That was not only proven during the war and all the bombings, that has also been proven scientifically. For example, the Jews today in Palestine know how to live with situations that they themselves . . . it is said that 50 percent say of themselves, "What is being done here is against all I believe in; I cannot agree to that." But nevertheless they stay there, because they say on the other hand, "It is for my people. It is for the higher principle, even though I might not agree with it."

OSTERMANN: Well, I must say, with the situation in Auschwitz or Ravensbrück [Women's concentration camp, established 1939 north of Berlin, until 1945 approximately 132,000 women and children were sent there, approximately 16,000 died there]—after all I have been through, a total of thirty-three months of incarceration, including Gestapo, etc.— I could never come to terms with these situations, even though I lived in that environment.

MÜNCH: Of course, you had no alternative.

OSTERMANN: That's just it. I had no alternative! You did!

MÜNCH: Yes, I had the alternative. But if I abandoned these people, that I could keep, with whom I had personal contact, if I handed them over, then on one hand I have soothed my conscience, on the other hand, burdened it. Of course, the matter came up in the large trial and weighed on my side. The women took care to talk everywhere about these experiments as very disagreeable, even inhumane. We really wanted a few to die.

OSTERMANN: Aha!

MÜNCH: . . . pro forma to die, you understand. Then we'd smuggle them out somehow. That was the plan. The officially known facts of that matter were brought out by the prosecution during the trial, of course with much pathos. And then . . .

OSTERMANN: I now have another question.

MÜNCH: Just a minute, please let me finish my story. At that time, when I was accused of the official version of the story, several women, not only one, several of them, stood up and said, "These were not the true facts; that was thus and thus . . . " And at the point the whole audience of that trial—and it was an important trial, believe me—that whole auditorium agreed with what was said in my favor.

OSTERMANN: Well, yes. If it would not have been for that matter, you would not have been acquitted.

MÜNCH: That is just what I am saying. All these things are so . . . We both started out by saying that we are inhibited about talking to each other or, shall we say, prejudiced . . .

OSTERMANN: No, I have no prejudice at all.

MÜNCH: I must admit I have some.

OSTERMANN: I am not prejudiced at all, or I would never have agreed to talk to you. Only if one is totally objective, without any prejudice, can one have a conversation with a former SS man who was, so to speak, involved in Auschwitz. I probably would not have agreed to a conversation with an SS man whom I knew to have been tried and convicted by a court of law. But what I would like to know at this point is how did you, from your position in the camp, rate your fellow SS men? What kind of people did you think they were?

THREE CATEGORIES OF PERPETRATORS
Obedient Slaves, Opportunists, and the True Believers

MÜNCH: Well, yes. You can imagine that one receives the shock of a lifetime, on seeing everything there for the first time. That is a given.

That you then ask yourself, how do they stand this? Why do they do it? How do they cope with it; that also is a given . . . And strangely enough, the solution is simple. Over time I observed three clearly identifiable categories. First, there are those who have been drilled to obey, soldierly obedience, a kind of slavish [unquestioning] obedience. Their ideal is to execute orders regardless of what the orders demand; this is the least comprehensible. The second category, which also played an important part in Auschwitz, were the blatant opportunists. You know certainly that Mr. Himmler promised his specially qualified concentration-camp soldiers heaven on earth and that he told them: "You have to do the most onerous work; you have to do things that demand a lot of steadfastness; that is why your role in the future of the Third Reich is going to be a unique one." There were quite a number of them who counted on these promises—and perhaps we have to include the doctors in this category; this category applies especially to them. And then there is the third category: the true believers. I cannot say how many of them have to be counted into this one, because it is hard to separate them out from the first and second category. They were the perpetrators by conviction. They were the ones who would say: "Part of my ideology is to destroy the inferior races, so that German heritage can become so powerful that it can restore the world to purity and health and mainly that then Germany can triumph over everything and everyone." That is the third category, and I have not noticed any other motivations that could be put into a category.

Category One

OSTERMANN: The first category, which you see as unquestioning obedience, I can easily understand, as long as I would not have to be confronted with the results of the orders I have followed obediently. But if someone sees the results of this obedience, maybe he would start thinking for himself after all, even if you represent him as primitive. Sometimes the primitive person has more heart than an intellectual who listens to his reason. That such a person would give unqualified obedience, in view of what he has to do, seems a little unbelievable to me. Otherwise, we would have to believe that all human beings who come into such a situation would do the same because they have been drilled into obedience. That would mean that Hitler has raised a child-like people, that he had deprived them of independent thinking, so that they would follow every order unquestioningly.

MÜNCH: That is just what I am saying. This is how it was. And it was not only Hitler who did that, that runs throughout the history of the world. The well-drilled soldier actually does everything as ordered. Otherwise he would be a bad soldier. And in earlier times he would be beastly punished even for the smallest infraction. Propaganda has worked hard later on to firm up this manner of manipulating human beings. You can find this kind of manipulation not only in the realm of the military but in every organized religion. If you think about all the inhuman orders and activities in the middle ages, such as burning witches, things that can not be understood by reason, that can only be ascribed to the force of propaganda, those are the facts that you simply cannot overlook. Mankind is obviously so primitive, and not much persuasion is needed to motivate them to this sense of slavish, unquestioning obedience. And now I have to reiterate what I said before: the absolutely primitive propaganda practiced by Hitler, together with the imposing spectacles, the perfectly arranged mass parades and party-days, like in Nuremberg, contributed considerably to break the people completely of independent thinking. According to this kind of obedience, a large number of the perpetrators active in Auschwitz gave that obedience priority above everything else, and one has to understand them from that point of view. I don't know how many of them were in that mode, because the motivations intersect here somewhat. And there you have the next motivation for many of them...

OSTERMANN: May I interrupt you briefly? Your comparison with all other military personnel leaves something to be desired. Because, if I today join the military and give my oath to unquestioning obedience, then I commit myself to defend my country if necessary, against an invisible enemy, as it happened many times during the war. But here in the camp, a man was forced to obedience and let himself be forced to murder the person in front of him. And that was someone who was

not only not an enemy but someone who had not lifted a finger against him. That is a totally different situation from drilling a soldier today to fight for his country if there should be a war. That is why I simply cannot imagine that those were people who came there on a normal path. If you say that this is a fact, you would have to assume that every German, being in the same situation, would commit the same atrocities? I would think your compatriots would reject that idea strongly, that given if they were in the same situation they would all commit these deeds. There would have been many who would have deserted and who would have said "no, I will not do that." And as I said before, they could do that. The things that have been done in the camp—I don't need to go into detail now; we know what we mean— the gassings, the punishments meted out and much more, the cruel- ties, the starvation, etc.—these were not normal actions of normal human beings. Therefore, those who did it simply had to be a different kind of animal.

MÜNCH: Not at all. You see that incorrectly and strictly from your point of view, your educational background, your way of thinking and feeling. People are different; they can be manipulated. You assert that I degrade all Germans. I will go a step farther. Not only the Germans can be manipulated, probably many other people would be subject to such manipulation as well. You see that proven time and again. It is no secret that Stalin practically starved and ruined three million or more of his own people, and not a soul protested against that . . .

OSTERMANN: But he always claimed judicial proceedings as an excuse.

MÜNCH: So what! Does that change anything about the facts? But you seem to be of the opinion that man is—to put it into the extreme—so decent that it is impossible to drill him into unquestioning obedience by pressure or pure propaganda. That is your . . . well, one cannot actually say, your experience.

OSTERMANN: My opinion.

MÜNCH: . . . your emotionally based opinion. From my experience I simply must contradict you, because I saw with my own eyes that that is not the case. Maybe, if I had never experienced Auschwitz, I might have seen it like you do. But you, as a victim of Auschwitz should really be able to see this much more than I.

OSTERMANN: What I want to say is that these people cannot be the normal people that you claim they are. Because a totally normal human being, even if you force him a thousand times to obedience, would in the face of facts like Auschwitz, react differently.

MÜNCH: So you say!

OSTERMANN: Yes, so I say . . .

MÜNCH: And I still claim that according to my experience it is obviously possible, because for these "totally normal people," there simply was no arguing. And of course we talked about that, with some of them at least, and they told me pointblank that it was as I thought. That is my experience.

OSTERMANN: . . . Apropos of this I would like to tell you a true case of my experience. I don't know if I already mentioned that my uncle on my mother's side was a long-time partymember, who had already joined in the 20s. As they used to say—an old campaigner. And believe me, if he would have been in that situation, he would not have lent himself to these goings-on, and he would have said, "No way will

I do that," in spite of his being an ardent national socialist. And my second uncle, who also was an "old campaigner" with the party, went with me to the Gestapo, because my mother had asked him to, when I was summoned. One of his comrades from the illegal time of the party was at that office, and my mother wanted her brother to ask him why they summoned me to the Gestapo. He went with me, and his comrade was very nice to him and asked what he could do for my uncle. My uncle said: "My niece here has received a summons. What do you want with her". And the official asked: "Did she do some-thing?" "No, no," my uncle said, "she did not do anything, but you remember that my sister was married to a Jew and Dagmar is so to speak a half-cast. Can you advise me what to do?" And his comrade said: "There is only one bit of advice I can give you, the best thing for her would be to hang herself." And do you know what my uncle's reaction was to that remark? He said, "Is that what I fought for, that you tell members of my family to hang themselves?" And in a wider sense, even if these people were drilled to unquestioning obedience when they saw what was expected of them, they could have readily said: "That is not what I fought for, to murder people in cold blood."

MÜNCH: I hope you understand that your uncle, if he would have been in the SS, would have never been selected for the category of the KZ units . . .

OSTERMANN: Well, now we have finally arrived at the sore point.

MÜNCH: . . . these people were carefully selected.

OSTERMANN: Right. They always chose people who showed a certain amount of brutality to start with.

MÜNCH: Just a minute. I am not going to say that they chose them for brutality exclusively. Most of them really did not act that brutal . . .

OSTERMANN: There too I have to contradict you . . .

MÜNCH: We are speaking of the guard detail, aren't we?

OSTERMANN: Of course, of the guard detail.

MÜNCH: You simply can't say that most of them were brutal. There was . . .

OSTERMANN: From my personal experience I can tell you a lot of things about those men.

MÜNCH: Oh well, I must agree; there I might not know quite as much.

OSTERMANN: Because believe me, SS men walked along the highway, and if there was a prisoner's nose they did not like, or perhaps his downtrodden posture, or perhaps the SS was just in a bad mood, they would blindly start beating that prisoner without any reason whatsoever, without . . .

MÜNCH: Ah well, What percentage of them were like that?

OSTERMANN: Believe me, the percentage was high, very, very high.

Category Two

OSTERMANN: Let us talk now about the second category, the SS elite, this group that the doctors belonged too, and to whom they promised God knows what.

MÜNCH: Not only the doctors were promised heaven on earth.

OSTERMANN: The higher-ups also?

MÜNCH: No, everyone, absolutely everyone was promised everything, across the board. That applied to the entire KZ-SS, let us say, to the inner circle, to all those who had to do with the extermination of the Jews.

OSTERMANN: Well, I guess they promised them all kinds of medals etc. I cannot imagine that normal thinking human beings could be influenced by any kind of authority or some generous promises, which might or might not be kept, to commit these kinds of cruelties, these inhumane actions. That shows again that these people could not have been normal humane people. There is no way that a man who thinks humanely, who has a heart, would lend himself to such deeds, in spite of pie-in-the-sky promises. Only a certain kind of human being is capable of that; you cannot change my mind about that.

MÜNCH: I am not trying to change your mind, but you asked me about my experience. If I would have to quantify it, I would have to say that at least one third of the people there were the kind of people who actually did what they did without any special conviction, merely because they were drilled to obey, to be a good soldier. It was part of being a soldier, to obey orders, that was all. I do not want to denigrate them or put any qualification on them at all. I simply want to say that was that category of men. You asked me about my experience and I have to say . . .

OSTERMANN: Actually I did not want to hear so much about your experience, rather I was interested in how you saw these people from your vantage point, how did it affect you that there were people who could do this sort of thing. You must have acknowledged their existence, even if you did not appreciate their actions.

MÜNCH: The experience touched me as a man and as a physician. I had to find out, for myself, whether such things existed at all, or whether it was just my imagination, and so I started talking to them. That was my kind of experience and, it would seem, that you simply can't accept that from your viewpoint, because your viewpoint is just different.

OSTERMANN: I cannot have a different viewpoint than the one I have. I have seen with my own eyes what happened there.

MÜNCH: You did not merely see it, you felt it, you suffered it, you understand that, don't you? I too suffered from a totally different point of departure, I suffered as one who belonged to that group, who was forced to go through experiences that he basically rejected, which were completely novel to him.

OSTERMANN: Let us change the subject. Let us talk about the doctors specifically.

MÜNCH: No, not yet, we'll get to that subject later anyway. But I specified three categories to you. Can we check off this category?

OSTERMANN: OK. We can check that one off.

MÜNCH: You still cannot accept my theory.

OSTERMANN: No, I cannot.

MÜNCH: Somehow or other, I don't seem to be able to prove it to you, or I would have to have an immense reservoir of experiences to convince you.

OSTERMANN: The main reason you cannot prove anything to me is because my argument is based on the purely humane point of view.

MÜNCH: I know.

OSTERMANN: . . . and as long as I base my argument on this point of view, I cannot accept your excuse.

MÜNCH: It is no excuse, it is an experience, a fact . . . a fact that I describe to everyone, not only you, everyone who asks me, how it was down there in Auschwitz, what kind of people they were. I don't pass judgment, not pro, not contra—let us leave it at that, otherwise we . . .

OSTERMANN: Otherwise we will just talk and talk . . .

MÜNCH: Not only talk and talk, but we will start philosophizing: What is justice? What is injustice? Better people have not been able to crack that hard nut. All right, let us continue to the category of the opportunists. They had an opportunistic attitude to the whole situation, i.e., well, now it is the turn of national socialism. Let's see how I can make the best of it for myself. Here I seem to be in the right spot and, I'll do what needs to be done accordingly. I don't really know how many of those there were. But among the so-called leaders, I am sure there were more of them than of the third category, the evildoers out of conviction.

OSTERMANN: We are not quite that far. I want to give you my view on the second category. You say that those opportunists were in agreement with the regime and its activities. But why did they agree?—because they knew that without that regime they would have never had a career.

MÜNCH: I don't really know that. I have seen some very qualified people, who even without . . .

OSTERMANN: If that was the case, than these people really had no need for opportunism. They could have proven their qualifications for their chosen career in very different circumstances and under different conditions. If I have the ability to be in a leading position, I can achieve that position by proving my ability for it; I don't have to necessarily prove myself by achievements in a KZ by stooping to murdering people. I just can't agree with you on that. These people chose the path of least resistance. They knew very well that by following orders, they opened up a successful career for themselves.

MÜNCH: That's right.

Category Three

OSTERMANN: And now we are ready for the third category.

MÜNCH: Yes, now we have arrived at the third category, they who committed these crimes out of real conviction, who were convinced that the Jews were our undoing, and who believed that even in the body of the German people there was racial contamination by Slavs or other non-Germanic nations.

OSTERMANN: You might as well add the Gypsies to the list.

MÜNCH: Of course the Gypsies, but there were others, more. Even among the pure Germans these people were convinced that the pure blondes were always the better people; they had no doubt about that. Whether that originated from their personal experience or whether they were taught such thinking, I cannot say. But they really acted out of pure conviction and belief. Believe me, I talked a lot with them, debated with them, and they loved to discuss their views. I know you are not a layperson, but what the simple layperson cannot understand is that it was possible to discuss such matters in Auschwitz, that it was possible even to have a different viewpoint, to talk against the prevailing view.

OSTERMANN: Oh, but I can well imagine that.

MÜNCH: You could of course, but the average, normal person, who has no personal experience with Auschwitz, has a hard time comprehending that. He only sees the SS as a totally intolerant gang, without any ideals, or, shall we say, philosophy of life. And it really was not like that at all. There were a large number of genuinely convinced perpetrators, just like there are fanatics in any religion. For example, in Christianity the most horrible crimes have been committed throughout history in the name of religion.

OSTERMANN: History, again?

MÜNCH: Well, sometimes it belongs to the topic. Evildoers by conviction exist and have existed throughout history; I can't even say how many, and here we have the third category.

OSTERMANN: Well, perhaps it is not even very important. But speaking of blue eyes and blond hair, which you just mentioned, I only have one thing to say. Among these so-called convinced perpetrators, from the leaders on down, I have not seen very many blue-eyed blondes. We could delve a bit more into these racial theories, but that would get us too far afield.

Perhaps we can discuss that at a later date. But right now, since we have finally arrived concretely at your part as SS doctor in Auschwitz,

I am interested in your scientific activities as SS doctor in the camp area. What kind of contact did you have with the other SS doctors?

MÜNCH: I really only had contact there with a few of the ones we just now categorized as evildoers by conviction; with the other ones I only had contact in an official capacity. They nauseated me. You see, I stayed away from them, as far as I could . . .

OSTERMANN: And mainly with these convinced ones you . . .

MÜNCH: Only with them did I have discussions, intensive discussions.

OSTERMANN: Name some of them.

MÜNCH: Well, there was, for example, an otherwise totally primitive man, i.e., Mengele.

OSTERMANN: Ah, Mengele.

MÜNCH: Yes, Mengele interested me extremely. Whenever I mention that fact, I am looked at rather askance, but I really know of some exculpating arguments, because he really was not in every respect as he is generally portrayed.

OSTERMANN: And how did his arguments go? How, for example did he justify his activities?

MÜNCH: He was convinced that if we failed to exterminate the Jews, to, so-to-speak, wipe them off the map, there would be no way that any people in the civilized European world could be governed properly, because the Jews would always have their fingers in the financial problems. That was the direction of his arguments, and you could not possibly talk him out of that.

OSTERMANN: What else did he have to say? What made him hate the Jews so intensely?

MÜNCH: Because the Jews have a mental attitude directly opposed to the German people and the German mentality. "Just look at their artistic expressions," he would say, "the things they produce. Look at those schizophrenic portraits and the kind of things they spread. Why? To persuade mankind to reject the really beautiful paintings, such as those in the churches. Or look at the literature they have written, what horrible things they have written about. There is absolutely no idealism left in their writings. They only love to deal with menage à trois."

OSTERMANN: He must have read some strange literature, nothing of Stefan Zweig, nothing by Thomas Mann. There were . . .

MÜNCH: But no, Mann was no Jew . . .

OSTERMANN: Obviously he was extremely narrowminded. He only picked out what displeased him.

MÜNCH: Wait, now we talk again about something that does not exist, don't we. Because we said "the Jew" per se, does not exist.

OSTERMANN: What was his attitude towards his guinea pigs? He made his experiments on human guinea pigs.

MÜNCH: There he had a rather strange rationale. He claimed that there was no problem for him. "The Jews in Auschwitz will certainly not survive, no question about that. And with every transport, there arrive a certain number of identical twins. There is no place in the world where one can experiment with identical twins. Why? Because these experiments are inhumane. Because you are not allowed to treat them," like—how did he phrase that—yes, "rabbits. Here we can do that" he said, "and if I do not select them out and use them for scientific purposes, then I really violate the oath that I have sworn."

OSTERMANN: So that is how he brought that in accord with the Hippocratic Oath?

MÜNCH: That is how he did it.

OSTERMANN: And that did not seem strange to you?

MÜNCH: I am not talking about that. We are not talking about me here.

OSTERMANN: But yes. You said yourself that he was one of the persons you liked to talk to, actually your preferred conversation partner . . .

MÜNCH: That is true. And just like you and I converse here, that is how I conversed with him, discussed things with him. "How can you justify that to yourself?" I would say. And he answered: "I don't have to justify anything to myself, I have only to justify it to the German People." And then he'd start on his well-known litany. Whether that was a psychological trick to exculpate himself, or whether he really believed it, that I don't know to this day.

OSTERMANN: Wasn't one of the reasons for your acquaintance that you did some scientific experimentations together?

MÜNCH: [emphatically] No, no, no.

ADJUSTING TO THE EXTERMINATION UNIVERSE
(MÜNCH)

Functions of the Hygiene Institute

OSTERMANN: I know quite well that some of the medical data were passed on to you. Your department also did examinations of sperm . . .

MÜNCH: No, no, . . .

OSTERMANN: I am afraid I have to contradict you once again. That prisoner still lives in Vienna today. She was impregnated in camp. She was an "Aryan" prisoner, as much as I dislike the word, but referring to Auschwitz, I guess one must use it. The child's father also was a prisoner, a German political prisoner, who tried to deny his paternity. Even Hössler was involved in the affair.

MÜNCH: Don't you mean Höss?

OSTERMANN: No, Hössler. He was the commanding officer of Auschwitz.

MÜNCH: I did not know him.

OSTERMANN: That male prisoner tried to implicate Hössler as the father. The woman whom he had impregnated tried to put the paternity onto Untersturmführer Hössler, because they knew that there could be severe punishment for the real father. Hössler, of course, rejected the accusation, and the sperm tests were ordered to determine paternity. Those tests were done in your institute.

MÜNCH: But that is not an experiment!

OSTERMANN: I just mention that because you just said that your institute did no sperm tests.

MÜNCH: But that is a routine matter.

OSTERMANN: I don't think that was a very common occurrence in Auschwitz. Surely you must remember it.

MÜNCH: No, that case I don't remember. There were hundreds of specimens sent for examination to the institute, every day, every single day. The institute was established for one reason, which was to inhibit the spread of epidemics beyond the camp fences. Because earlier—I don't think you were there yet—if there was found to be typhoid fever spreading in a barrack, then that barrack was closed, do you understand what I mean . . . ?

OSTERMANN: Sure, I was there in those times. You forget that I came to Auschwitz in October 1942. The big crematoria did not exist then. There was a typhoid epidemic, because I myself . . .

MÜNCH: Well yes, but the phase that I am talking of happened earlier. At that time, they simply closed the barracks, sent all the inhabitants to the gas, disinfected the structure, and put new prisoners into it.

OSTERMANN: I was there to see that, believe me.

MÜNCH: That, of course, led to cases where things were hushed up. Even to the extent that prisoner doctors would give deadly injections to people whom they knew to be infected with typhus, just so that not the whole barrack would march to the gas. That was the reason that the camp requested this institute. The institute did try to combat the epidemics somewhat with the existing means, as it is done normally.

OSTERMANN: But there is a contradiction there. The big crematoria were not build until sometime during 1943. Before that, there was only the small crematorium in Auschwitz I and the farmhouses, far behind the then men's camp in Birkenau, which had been restructured to serve as gaschambers. There were no crematoria at that time; corpses were burned in ditches. The two farmhouses are still there to this day, but they were only used until crematoria 2, 3, 4, and 5 were running fulltime. The epidemics suited the SS and the government big shots quite well. They decimated the camps as planned.

MÜNCH: That is right. It was not the camp they were worried about.

OSTERMANN: And they did not make a big secret out of it. Remember what was written on the barracks: One louse, your death!

MÜNCH: Of course the institute's work did not serve the prisoners, but the personnel [troops]. It started with the wife of SS Obersturmbann-führer Caesar. She contracted typhoid fever; she had worked with prisoners, had been in contact with them, and there was great fear that the infection could spread to the city of Auschwitz where the civilians and personnel lived. That is why the institute was brought here, not for humanitarian reasons—for the prisoners.

OSTERMANN: I really would have doubted that . . .

MÜNCH: I never claimed that it was for the prisoners' sake.

OSTERMANN: Certainly not for humanitarian reasons. During those times, the main concern for the SS was how quickest to decimate the prisoners, whether by epidemics or by injections.

MÜNCH: But a stop was put to that pretty soon, and quarantine wards were started because the workforce was badly needed.

OSTERMANN: Well, it was not quite that soon. I came to Birkenau in October 1942, from Ravensbrück. Since I came with a mixed transport of Jews and half-Jews, we were not selected at the ramp, but sent directly into the camp. They first had to register us, so that if one of these half-Jews would die, their Aryan or Christian relatives could be informed. That is why we came into the camp before selection, and only after we had been tattooed and shaved and deprived of our Ravensbrück prisoner clothing were we selected. I don't remember the name of the doctor who did it. The second SS man whom I noticed there was Unterscharführer Erber. I remember him because I saw him later in the Political Section, when I worked there. At that time, those selected for the gas were sent to block 25, the so-called collection block for the ones to be gassed. That block also collected the ones selected for the gas from the working commandos as they marched out in the morning. [Trans. note: Also at the return from daily work during early 1943]. There were daily selections, not always on a large scale. Sometimes in small numbers like our transport. Those who were not selected for the gas went into the barracks.

MÜNCH: Those were the first rather primitive measures of quarantine. Later of course . . .

OSTERMANN: Those were no measures of quarantine. These people were murdered immediately. They were collected in block 25. And when block 25 was full, they would throw out the ones who already had died in the block. That was my first impression when I arrived in Birkenau. It was still fairly dark, only shadowy outlines were visible. We had to line up along the fence, and opposite us I saw these barracks. And in front of one of these barracks I saw a very big heap of something, that in the faint light, looked like treetrunks. Only with daylight did I realize what I was looking at: a heap of corpses. Those were the corpses thrown out of block 25 to make room for the newly arrived, selected women. But if the block filled up too quickly, the living and the dead were loaded indiscriminately on the truck and ferried to the gaschambers. There was not a hint of a quarantine.

MÜNCH: That's just what I said.

OSTERMANN: At that time the women's camp in Birkenau was section BIa separated by two wire fences from the men's camp, section BIb. Only later, a whole year later, the women's camp became the so-called quarantine camp, but you could not really call it a quarantine camp. BIa and BIb were joined into the so-called labor camp for women, and the men were transferred elsewhere. That is how Birkenau developed. I must add, however, that all in all, I was rather lucky.

MÜNCH: You almost had to have some luck to survive at all.

OSTERMANN: Right. Because while we were standing at that fence waiting for daylight, and to find out what would happen to us, an Oberscharführer came along. He had a list and read out the names on it in alphabetical order. And since my maiden name was "Bock" and he was already at the letter "K," I said, "Excuse me, sir, but you did not read my name." And he asked my name and I said, such and such, and he looked at the list and said, "But you are not on the list." And since I was rarely at a loss for an answer, I said, "OK, in that case you can send me home again." And that was my luck. By that answer and the fact of not being on the list, I was taken out of a transport of 522 women and girls. The SS man said to me, "Stand over there on the side." Of course I did not know why he did that; he did not tell me. And then came the above mentioned Unterscharführer, whom at that time I did not know by name. You could not help but remember him. He had very thick, black eyebrows and simply looked cruel. The two SS men whispered with each other and kept pointing at me; I did not know what it was all about. And then we were tattooed, and I was one of the last ones of that transport to be tattooed (No. 21946). And as I passed the SS men, Oberscharführer Stark (I learned his name later on), seeing my long, blonde, "Aryan" hair, said, "What a pity for that beautiful hair." Then we were led to the back of the building and shaved bald, and then came the aforementioned selection, where we had to march stark naked past the the SS doctor and that Unterscharführer who had whispered with him. I was lucky enough to be sent to the side of the living. Later on I was assigned to the so-called Jewish blocks, you know those brick buildings. As you well know, the so-called administrative prisoners and the Aryan prisoners were housed on the other side of the camp street in the prefabricated, wooden barracks, and we were in the brick blocks, with . . .

MÜNCH: With those long things . . .

OSTERMANN: Yes, with those bunks. And the next morning, of course, came the roll call. Already during the night I had accumulated hundreds of lice. After the roll call, we were dragged immediately to work on an outside commando, because the Kapos were in a hurry to collect their commandos for the marching out. I was put into the commando called "Tree Nursery," where we had to uproot and transplant trees. Anyway, after we marched back in in the evening and after the usual roll call, I heard my number called in the barrack by the block leader. I really did not yet identify with my number at that time, and all of a sudden my name was called also, and this Unterscharführer, named Erber, as I later found out, who looked so frightfully cruel, yelled at me and then said, "You were not supposed to march out at all. You stay in camp tomorrow. Blockleader, I hold you responsible for her." But no one bothered to tell me any reason for that. I already thought, perhaps they will shoot me, because I had opened my big mouth. This was another example of the sadistic streak in those people, not to tell the prisoner, "You are staying in camp tomorrow, because you are selected for a certain job."

MÜNCH: But you must have known you were not considered a human being at that moment. You were just a number.

OSTERMANN: That's right, just a number. And so without any further explanation, I was ordered not to march out the next day, and the blockleader hid me carefully right after roll call, so that I would not be shanghaied by some Kapo into an outside commando. Then a young girl came to the block. She was dressed better. You could see she had been in camp already for a while. She said, "You are coming with me." And I said, "Where to?" And she said, "you are going into the main office." And so I worked for a short time in the main office where the new arrivals were being registered. That office was a subdivision of the Political Section. But in that section I did not stay very long. On the second day of working there, Oberscharführer Stark came and said: "You are going to work in Auschwitz [the main camp]." So I received some prisoner clothing and was transferred to another block. When I was transferred to the main office, I was also immediately transferred out of the brick block to another block—one of the wooden prefab blocks, which were cleaner and also had washing facilities. I also got a change of clothing. That did not happen for humanitarian reasons, but only because in the office you came in contact with the SS, and clean clothes and cleaner surroundings reduced the danger of contamination for them. What neither they nor I knew at the time was that I already had spotted fever. So now I had the striped prisoner clothing and had to march to Auschwitz every morning and back every evening, because there was no housing for office workers in the main camp. Some days I ran a high fever and only due to the care of my fellow prisoners could I keep working in spite of sickness. They practically pulled me out of bed every morning, saying, "You are not staying in bed." Because they knew only too well that staying in bed could mean being caught in a selection and going to the gas. They rubbed some red paper (or something else red) on my cheeks and supported me as we marched out— we were not a very big commando—so that no one would notice that I was burning with fever. And I walked the three and one-half kilometers to Auschwitz every day. And at this point I must add that there were some men who were not so totally devoted to unquestioning obedience. There was an SS man who was our escort, the man Pyschny, whom I mentioned before, who never got any kind of promotion until the end of '45 [she must mean '44]. He could well see that I was feverish and was staggering—after all it is hard to disguise such a condition for 3–3 1/2 kilometers—and he never reported me. Thank God, I survived the spotted fever without missing a day of work or staying in the block. How I did it, I'll never know. It was probably due to my strong constitution and my determination to stay alive. And one day when we came back to Birkenau, there was great excitement in the camp. There had been a large, horrendous selection. That was in December '42.

MÜNCH: Wasn't that in 1943?

OSTERMANN: No, it was December '42. That is documented. When we wanted to get into our block, we were told, "No need to go in there. The beds have been torn apart; the strawsacks have been emptied, everything is being fumigated." We had to completely undress and throw our clothes onto a heap. "They will also be fumigated." And then something happened that again showed the blatant sadism surpassing any given order. We had to march to the men's camp. The gates between the two camps had been opened (between BIa and BIb); normally they were locked. We had to walk on top of a long bench and male prisoners—who probably hadn't seen a woman for years or perhaps only for months, depending on how long they had been in the camp, shaved us everywhere—including the pubic hair. Then we were led into a real sauna that had been installed in the men's camp. Perhaps they were trying to make us sweat out all the disease germs. Then, walking through a door again, we were once more confronted by men, who sprayed us with some kind of disinfectant—I really don't know what was left to spray at. Then we came under a cold shower and then had to wait, stark naked, outside for our clothes. That, of course, lasted for hours. Many people died from exposure, after having been in the hot sauna, the cold shower, and then standing outside naked in December with terribly weakened bodies ... So now we waited for our clothing, and then we went back to our block, had to put up the beds again, and stuff the strawsacks. And that was exactly what you had talked about. The blocks were closed; the people were sent to the gas. At that date not only one block, but many, many blocks were closed. I might even say that all the blocks were subjected to the selection.

MÜNCH: Yes, and it was the Hygiene Institute that prevented a recurrence of such events.

OSTERMANN: The selections did not stop because of the Institute's activities.

MÜNCH: Perhaps the selections in general did not stop, but they stopped selecting and gassing entire barracks. But we really do not want to talk about that, because ...

OSTERMANN: But that is very important. The experience we had in the men's camp made it obvious how they totally humiliated and mortified women. Not merely the fact that a human being . . .

MÜNCH: You are still going on the assumption that the SS saw the prisoners as human beings. That is what makes this so interesting. You yourself have suffered all these humiliations, and you still assume, somehow, that in Auschwitz the prisoners were human beings. They were numbers, nothing else. And if one tries to comprehend Auschwitz—which is practically impossible—that fact is almost a precondition.

OSTERMANN: That again is proof positive that only a certain kind of people were posted to Auschwitz: people who lacked all humanity, who did not look at their fellow men as human beings. It seems we cannot progress beyond this point. But we still have not arrived at my actual reason for agreeing to this conversation.

MÜNCH: We do have plenty of time.

OSTERMANN: I wanted you to speak about your personal perceptions. I would like you to allow me an insight into you as a man; what did you feel? What was your position vis-à-vis that whole matter, your thinking, your emotions? That should be the crux of this conversation, otherwise I really don't see any need for this talk with you. The facts of Auschwitz I know only too well.

MÜNCH: I am afraid I have to disappoint you. I have repeatedly told you that the whole situation repelled me horrendously. Why I remained there nevertheless, I have tried already to explain to you. I was firmly convinced that I—under the conditions that I secured there for myself with great difficulties—by managing to stay out of any criminal activities, could be of great help as a physician. What would have been achieved if I had left there? I would have been assigned to some field laboratory and might have survived the war, or not. My leaving would not have changed the existence of Auschwitz for one moment. But you want to find out about emotions. I realize there is always somewhere a key experience that gives a closer clue to the matter. To describe my emotions is simply not my style; that is very very difficult.

OSTERMANN: I have the feeling you are side-stepping the issue a bit.

MÜNCH: Of course I am evading a bit; I can't express it precisely.

OSTERMANN: Let me put it a bit more concretely. I am going to ask you a purely personal question: At that time you already had a child of your own. And you knew very well that thousands of children went into the gas, innocent children who had never harmed anyone and of whom no one would ever know what they might have achieved as adults. You were a father yourself. Did it never occur to you how you would feel if that would happen to your child?

MÜNCH: Of course it did. But how can I describe these feelings to you?

OSTERMANN: That should be easy, anyone can describe his innermost feelings.

MÜNCH: No, no, that was horrible, frightful, atrocious. But words can not describe anything like that. What happened to the children, that was a totally incomprehensible experience; one cannot even talk of emotions . . .

OSTERMANN: Why don't you say inhuman instead of incomprehensible, because that's what it was . . .

MÜNCH: I know, I know, but what does that mean, that does not express it. Those are merely words . . .

OSTERMANN: But the word "inhuman" is surpassingly applicable for the events at Auschwitz.

MÜNCH: Inhuman. That can cover a multitude of matters that are much less . . .

OSTERMANN: You were going to cite an example . . .

MÜNCH: I want to tell you of a key experience there, something that happened to me during the first few days in Auschwitz. As I had mentioned, I had gone to school in Dresden, and during an important developmental period of my puberty or prepuberty I had a friend, a Jewish friend, Leo Oppenheimer. He and I took a bicycle tour to Paris from Dresden. We did lots of things together; we were very good friends. During the first few days in Auschwitz, I stood at the gate at the men's camp and watched the labor columns march in. I moved a bit closer to the columns, so I could observe the process. I was the new one, and no one spoke to me. There I stood and watched, and for the first time I became aware of the incredible misery of these people. All of a sudden I saw Leo Oppenheimer in one of the columns. From that moment on I could think of nothing else but how to get Leo out, but I had no idea of how to go about that. That was the first time I got blind drunk. A few days later—by now I had become acquainted with some of the non-commissioned personnel who belonged to that particular commando—I had some drinks with one of the Austrians from the group, and the first thing I asked him was, "How can I possibly get in touch with that prisoner?" And he said, "For God's sake, don't be crazy. If you want to do him some good, don't dare to ask for his name or number in the Political Department. That could only harm him. You have to find some other way to get information. Ask some prisoners. I know a few people. I shall find out his number for you, and we shall go from there. But, never, never ask through official channels. Otherwise, they'll accuse you of trying to make contact with prisoners." I had been told the same thing already at the commander's office, but he confirmed it for me. So the man really tried but could not find out anything. Later on I had some pretty good connections myself, and I probably could have found his number if it really were Leo Oppenheimer. But I guess it was not him I had seen; I never saw him again. It is possible that he never was there, and in my subconscious I thought I saw him. But in my agitated condition at that time, I was convinced that I had seen him. Can you understand that? That was for me a deeply moving experience, and I cannot find words to express the emotions. That was a personal, human experience that I had there. Everything else happened among such masses of faceless prisoners, it became quite abstract.

OSTERMANN: Perhaps it was abstract for you, for us it was starkly concrete.

MÜNCH: Of course, of course it was for you, standing on the other side. For me the situation was very abstract, much less personal. At that time I had not yet seen any children being selected for the gas. Suppressing emotions is really not all that bad under such circumstances, it became a matter of survival. If one would be incapable of doing that in many situations, especially emotional situations, one could go insane.

OSTERMANN: Let me tell you something. It was already at that time in your power to officially ask about your friend. You could have requested him for your department. You told me yourself how many you managed to save by requesting them for the experiments.

MÜNCH: But you first had to have connections to do that.

OSTERMANN: You confided your key experience to me. But nevertheless I want to press you a bit more. Look at me; here I am, a victim. And though my experiences in Auschwitz were anything but good, I can freely talk about my emotions, about everything that I felt then, that I feel now. Why is it that you cannot do that, that you are incapable of that? For me as a victim, it cannot be any easier than for you who actually stood apart from the events, who was not directly involved. Why do you build a wall around yourself? You do, you know. You do not let me see your innermost thoughts, then or now. There must be a way to break through your reserve. People can talk about their feelings; I am doing it, and my position is certainly not the easier one.

MÜNCH: But you are in an easier position; you are a victim. You were mistreated, beaten, kicked.

OSTERMANN: You don't really think that this conversation is easier for me than for you.

MÜNCH: But I do believe just that. Because after all I am one of those responsible for it all. First of all, because I stayed there, and secondly, because I volunteered to start with—though only for the army. I do—to put it bluntly—have a bad conscience. I have to live with that, cope with that, and mainly, while in Auschwitz, I had to somehow come to terms with that bad conscience. I cannot possibly describe the many sleepless nights that I spent wrestling with these inner conflicts. That is so much more difficult . . .

OSTERMANN: But why can't you do that. Don't you think that if you talk things out, you help yourself emotionally?

MÜNCH: How can I describe my feelings to a person whom I meet today for the first time? As I said, words are insufficient. Figures also do not suffice, even if one tried to quantify the experience, such as, how many nights did you not sleep. You see that, don't you? Many people drowned all that in alcohol. I didn't do that, I was not capable of doing that. The impact of all that went much, much deeper. There are

things that one simply cannot talk about; perhaps it is also an indication of one's character. Some people are more introverted and others can open themselves up to the world. I can only speak of my experiences and impressions, not my emotions. The emotions were so deeply hurt . . . you mentioned the example of the children . . . if one felt in any shape or form . . .

OSTERMANN: . . . confronted with that . . .

MÜNCH: . . . responsible for that, then talking about emotions is out of the question, because there are no words in our language to express them; albeit one is an exceptionally gifted writer or a man who . . . I simply cannot do it. I am basically a man of science, objective, scientifically trained. I cannot think or act differently. I cannot describe emotions.

OSTERMANN: I just can't imagine that someone like you, who considers himself an intellectual . . .

MÜNCH: But that has nothing to do with intellect.

OSTERMANN: . . . can't express in his mother tongue what he feels. That is why man was given language, so that he may express his thoughts and feelings. Why can't you simply say, "This and this I felt. On such a night I could not sleep." That is what I would like to hear from you, just once. I still have not heard a single mea culpa, an admission that your innermost feelings were touched.

MÜNCH: But I have been saying nothing else. I have not been talking of anything else. Already with my first words, that I feel inhibited talking to a Jewish person, I used the expression "bad conscience." I always have felt self-conscious, I have said that from the start. And even now, I cannot bring myself to say that I am essentially guilty.

OSTERMANN: Well, you did belong to a so-called criminal organization.

MÜNCH: But that does not mean that much. If that were so [belonging to a criminal organization], then all Catholics who burned witches would have to . . .

OSTERMANN: Well, here we are again in the middle ages.

MÜNCH: . . . yes, would have to be marked as criminal organizations. It is not that simple; one cannot cope with such occurrences. Those are matters that fate has written. It is easy for you to talk as a victim.

OSTERMANN: Isn't that a rather lame comparison, the inquisition? The inquisition did not destroy a large part of humanity with organizational and bureaucratic efficiency. What happened in Auschwitz is unique in human history.

MÜNCH: Now we are straying into philosophy. It is true that masses were mechanically gassed, but first they had been destroyed ideologically. The requirement for the ideological destruction was an ideological concept, a so-called ideological concept.

OSTERMANN: It is a good thing you said "so-called."

MÜNCH: It must be clear to you by now that I did not approve of the SS and its entire concept. That must have become clear from the fact that I joined them under really unfortunate circumstances. But my subsequent experiences in Auschwitz aroused some rather controversial sentiments in me. That probably sounds somewhat incredible, but I feel I must tell you more about this frame of mind, specifically.

OSTERMANN: I would be grateful to you if you would tell me any kind of experience from that time.

MÜNCH: Quite, quite. Perhaps that might help us, or rather, might help you, to gain some insight into my situation. Your feelings vis-à-vis the SS are totally unequivocal, one-dimensional; you only experienced one aspect of them. Let me try to give you another example.

OSTERMANN: Go ahead . . .

MÜNCH: After I had managed to extricate myself from having to do selections, they still continued to be short of manpower, i.e., doctors who would be willing to select. The task became unmanageable during the Hungarian transports. You know yourself how many came at that time. They came night and day, and there was almost no way to cope with these masses. At that time a young man was assigned to the Institute, fresh from the Junkerschule [elite military school], of course, already commissioned as lieutenant, a physician by the name of Delmotte. I can't remember his first name . . .

OSTERMANN: Unimportant.

MÜNCH: Anyway, he was assigned to us and was supposed to take over the task that I would have had to do . . .

OSTERMANN: You were supposed to.

MÜNCH: Yes, which I had refused. And when he returned from his first time inside the camp, he was absolutely destroyed, spiritually broken; it is hard to describe his state. And when he was told what he was supposed to do [select], that finished him. He locked himself in his room and would not talk to anyone. He was absolutely aghast with the reality of Auschwitz. In his Junkerschule they only taught him the ideals of the SS and about the soldierly virtues of the Waffen-SS. He had learned, of course, that the Jews were our undoing, and he accepted the fact that Himmler's racial theories were part of the SS religion, and he had accepted all that unquestioningly. But when he saw the practical applications of these theories, all his enthusiasm for the SS was destroyed. They simply could not use him at the ramp, and all the people who saw him felt sorry for him and said, "He will need a lot of help to get adjusted." He had a very impressive family background; he came from a highly qualified SS family. I don't know all the details. I only know that he immediately called his relatives. But he was not transferred out, he was told he would have to get used to it. He was assigned to a camp physician . . .

OSTERMANN: I heard of that case.

MÜNCH: . . . and was only assigned to duty for a few hours at a time so he would get used to it. He was sent to the camp hospital in the main camp [Auschwitz I]. They had a well staffed hospital there by comparison with the Birkenau hospitals.

OSTERMANN: Are you speaking of Auschwitz?

MÜNCH: Yes, the Auschwitz main camp.

OSTERMANN: You mean to say Auschwitz I.

MÜNCH: In that hospital they performed some relatively professional operations, depending of course on the materials available.

OSTERMANN: I am somewhat skeptical of that statement . . .

MÜNCH: Anyway, he could cope with that situation and accept it. Soon it was pointed out to him that if they do not select in the hospital, i.e., select those who would die of their diseases anyway, then some other prisoners, who might be cured, were prevented from obtaining care in the hospital. I am sure you have heard that kind of argumentation often enough; I don't have to tell you about it. The SS physician would be presented with a list of names; these are incurable, right, and the other ones still have hope. So they broke him in slowly. He was told, "If you are at the front and there is a battle, and there are wounded whom you must care for, and some of the wounded are Russians or other enemies, you also have to make a selection." In this devious way, they convinced him cynically that it was the job of a military physician that you do not treat every sick person to the best of your ability, but that you must decide which one to send on, which one to treat, and which one to disregard. That is how they trained him, step-by-step, for his job. I watched how this young man, no more than twenty years old, changed slowly and how within a short time—I don't remember whether it was three or four weeks, or only two weeks—he accepted the job of selecting.

OSTERMANN: At the ramp also?

MÜNCH: Yes, at the ramp as well. But he was nearly deranged, lost all touch with his surroundings, and never confided in anyone, not me either. He knew that I had rejected the service at the ramp. We once talked about it, and he admitted that his attachment to his family was especially depressing to him. I experienced his inner conflict at close range. They gave him all sorts of privileges to keep his morale up. They even brought his wife into the camp to be with him . . .

OSTERMANN: At this point I would really like to know, what did this whole affair with Delmotte mean to you?

MÜNCH: I am trying to explain to you that I saw the SS not merely as you or any other outsider would see them, but as one who knew more of the inner workings. I am well aware of the KZ SS man who, in his brutality, could not even qualify for the words "human being" anymore, because he was willing to commit unspeakable acts. Of course, in the beginning I also had no comprehension of the SS mentality, and I saw them all as tarred with the same brush. But it didn't take long to see that some of them were pure opportunists; we talked about that before, and some of them were dull, unquestioning order takers. And slowly, through closer acquaintance with some of them, I found out that, even among the ideologically convinced perpetrators, there were differences. Men like Delmotte, who had received special schooling in an elite SS school, had learned to repress matters that they actually should have been aware of, because they had to see that if the plan was the extermination of the Jews, killing them—in one way or the other—had to be part of the plan. But that is exactly what happened to me and many other Germans. We simply could not believe that the things written about in the *Völkische Beobachter* and by Streicher in his newspaper would actually become reality in the form that they did. We all managed to repress that. Even in the uppermost ranges of the SS elite, such as the one that produced Delmotte, that reality had been successfully repressed or shall we say, hidden under a blanket that one dare not lift up. The SS ideology was, as you know, structured in the form of a religion. There were all kinds of rituals, such as, the death's-head ring and all these items. They were on the way to becoming an actual religion. Even if I did not learn too much history in school, one thing had stayed with me. Religion had introduced much cruelty and inhumanity into the world, and the world, throughout history, had accepted that in the name of religion.

OSTERMANN: Question . . . Did this man Delmotte—or whatever his name was—have no problems, then, in accepting everything, the selections?

MÜNCH: I did not observe him anymore myself, but I can well imagine, from other examples I saw, that he might have behaved with exceeding brutality in the camp. I can well imagine that he did that out of sheer insecurity, out of his inner desperation, out of a nagging conscience. He could not afford to be seen as humane by the prisoners. There again you have a perfect example of the one-dimensional view the prisoners had of the SS. Why? Simply because they could not see the motivations behind the behavior.

OSTERMANN: How did you see Auschwitz as a whole, with all its Muselmänner and everything that physically and mentally assaulted you there?

MÜNCH: Well, as I have told you, I had enlisted with a sort of high idealism as a soldier and then landed in this inferno of Auschwitz. As a physician alone I could not comprehend how human beings could be dehumanized to that extent. I had to come to terms psychologically and physiologically with the basic concepts of the camp, starting with the most basic one, that of the Muselmann. I had to witness the fact that human beings were not only reduced to numbers, but that they could be manipulated like so many inanimate objects. That they would be judged purely on their usefulness: Can he/she still work, or should we burn them right away? To comprehend these incomprehensible facts was so monstrous that it is very difficult for me to describe my feelings about this process. One's feelings, one's emotions were totally overtaxed. When I arrived in Auschwitz, my emotions were well balanced, and suddenly my emotions as well as my reasoning were overstressed. I was there for some eighteen months. And later on, I saw things somewhat differently than at the beginning. That was the result of a certain numbing of the emotions, as well as habit and the experience of a kind of camaraderie among the staff. As I have mentioned,

I had good relations within our commando, and I enlarged those contacts also to the camp in general.

OSTERMANN: I wonder, how is it possible that one can become numb in the face of such suffering? The word "numbing" really irritates me because I cannot understand how one can become numb where the suffering never diminished.

MÜNCH: Oh, one can, one can. There are many examples of behavior in extreme situations. Whole books have been written about that. Habit takes over. Certain details that appear to be horribly shocking at the start, you begin to see from a different angle. For example, when one sees a Muselmann, one might have arrived at a point of view where it is simple to say: "Poor soul, . . . he looks like he will not make it much longer." Not too long ago one might not have felt that casual. We could debate a whole night about that point. But rest assured, many people have thought about that phenomenon, and I have experienced it myself. A certain numbing does inevitably occur. But there is another point of view that changes because one has more contact with the individuals. This viewpoint developed very strongly in my case. I headed a relatively small commando with approximately 100 men, and thus I knew everything about them, where they were from, what their family background was. That did change one's view of Auschwitz, though not very much. Later on, in conversations with some of the prisoners, I gained more insights that also changed my view of Auschwitz. I must tell you of another example in this context. It deals with a very important man in the Auschwitz hierarchy, i.e., Caesar, the head of the agriculture department. I don't remember his rank, probably Sturmbannführer, Obersturmbannführer? In my eyes that was a very high rank, and I stayed away from that kind. When I saw four stars and a cord on the shoulders, that was a good reason for me to keep my distance. There was always the chance that he could be one of the really evil ones. He must have gotten all those promotions through merit, and that he could only have obtained in the KZ, or he had to be one of the old, old campaigners. But then I ran into him in the American prison camp. The Americans were delighted to have caught such a big fish, and he, like myself, was about to be

handed over to Poland for his trial. That was in '46. I remember clearly
that the train stopped for a night and half a day, and all of a sudden,
word of mouth ran through the train that they had taken Caesar out.
They did not hand him over to the Poles after all. "Well," I thought
to myself, "that goes to show that they might have some use on their
side for such a bigwig." Right after the war, shortly after I had returned home, he appeared on my doorstep, the former
Obersturmbannführer, and "very important person" in Auschwitz,
Mr. Caesar. And he wants to know, "How did it go in Poland? How
did they treat you? I am still waiting for them to get me. What do
you think will happen to me?" etc., etc. And I could only tell him
what I had learned in the meantime from the examining magistrate
during my interrogation, namely: that against this highly decorated
and important Auschwitz participant—after all he was in charge of
approximately 1000 or perhaps even 2000 prisoners in his camp—
there were no charges. The reason for that was that Caesar had, from
way back, been one of the intimate friends of Himmler. And as a
young man he was very active in the movement. And when this
ideology became preoccupied with Germanity and the Jews, he was
one of the men who was deeply involved in that. But relatively soon,
he bailed out because he could not stomach it. He did remain in the
SS, because he accepted quite a few of the SS ideologies and also
thought, "If I stay with it, I can perhaps, because of my low membership number and my connections to Himmler, try to limit some
of the excesses." But, of course, that attitude was not appreciated
and pretty soon, right at the beginning of the war, he was simply put
out to pasture, literally, to his old profession. He had studied agriculture and was very interested in that field. They sent him to the Ukraine
to an experimental station working on rubber production from
dandylion juice.

OSTERMANN: That was before Auschwitz, wasn't it?

MÜNCH: Yes. In the Ukraine, before Auschwitz. And when the situation
there turned a bit risky because the station was located rather far East,
he had to leave. But his experiments had been fairly successful, so
they decided to have him finish them up. They had the idea to give

him a chance to work in Auschwitz. He could use the acreage there for the experiments, and they furnished a lab for him. When he arrived there and saw where he was (at that time he had never seen a KZ yet) he said, "This is no place for me; I will not stay here." When he realized that he had no choice he said, "I want my own camp." That's when they gave him that camp [Rajsko, the agricultural camp, where the Hygiene Institute was also located]. He ran that camp according to his principals. He decided how much food each prisoner received; essentially, he had arranged there a bearable . . .

OSTERMANN: Climate

MÜNCH: . . . climate, that's right. There was no way that the Poles could have accused him of any inhumanities, except for the fact that he was there. And with this I come to a very important point. This is where the Eastern nations—in this case the Poles and perhaps even the Russians—differed in their judgment of war criminals. From the American point of view, anyone who was somehow connected with the Nazis and was in any kind of position of decision making, was automatically marked as . . .

OSTERMANN: Of course, because the Americans said that the SS is a criminal formation.

MÜNCH: They went even farther than that—even a bureaucratic counselor who only sat behind the desk was also imprisoned. They said de facto, "Anyone who belonged to a criminal organization, such as the SS, is guilty."

OSTERMANN: I still would like an answer to my previous question: What can you tell me of your personal experience of Auschwitz? What were some of the details of that?

MÜNCH: Yes, the details are important, because one simply cannot generalize it. But one can get lost in all the details. There were so many impressions to cope with. To begin with, as I said before, I almost could not handle the way I saw human beings being degraded, dehumanized.

OSTERMANN: Are you talking of the psychological terror?

MÜNCH: You might call it that. Yes, and, of course, the effectiveness of that depended on the physical condition of the individual prisoner. Psychological terror was so effective because the normal prisoner was too undernourished and physically debilitated to start with, so that he had no possibility to react against that psychological terror. That was my impression of this method. Because observing the details, you would notice how at the rollcall the people would stand for hours and submit to all the bullying and torments. That to me was incomprehensible. The only way I could explain this phenomenon was that obviously the prisoners were physically and mentally debilitated by hunger.

OSTERMANN: And how did this physical debilitation impact on you? What did you feel when you saw these undernourished stick figures, more dead than alive? What did the man, the physician feel at that moment?

MÜNCH: Of course, I immediately comprehended intellectually that this was the system and that was the way their death was being expedited. It took a while until I comprehended the extent of that extermination machine, how it functioned together.

OSTERMANN: Obviously you never had the idea: Perhaps I could help here? Perhaps there is a way to heal some of these unfortunates. Did you even try at any time?

MÜNCH: Of course not. It would have been absurd to believe that as one of the little cogs, who came there to do some hygiene work, I could change the system.

OSTERMANN: You knew already, then, what the system was?

MÜNCH: That was self-evident.

OSTERMANN: And when you learned of the gassings the first time?

MÜNCH: They explained it this way: "Who is not useful anymore goes through the chimney." That was the first time I heard the word "selection" being used. I only learned later that selections already were done upon arrival. And the worst incomprehensible fact was that they counted the children on arrival simply as not useful and sent them to the gas. These are things one cannot describe, simply indescribable.

OSTERMANN: Could you cope with all that?

MÜNCH: I did ... of course I did ... But I cannot describe how I managed to do it.

OSTERMANN: Especially since you were the father of a child yourself.

MÜNCH: Strangely enough, that did not figure much into the situation. I asked myself often enough whether that was of any importance at the time. But it really wasn't. Because one must differentiate between what has personal meaning for you in the situation you witness and what you merely register as cruelty in general. It is difficult to separate the two. But seeing, or believing to see, a friend, whom I hadn't seen for ages, marching by in a prisoner column, that moved me much more than the general misery of the camp.

OSTERMANN: And what about the gassings, when you found out that not only sick people were gassed . . .

MÜNCH: I'll gladly tell you.

OSTERMANN: . . . but that at the arrival ramp perfectly healthy people went into the gas.

MÜNCH: Here I'll have to get back to Delmotte once more. I did not come into the camp with any kind of illusion. You would have thought that I was quite shocked by the reality. Strangely enough, in comparison with Delmotte, I was not. For him the world crumbled, because of the idealism that he brought with him from his elite education.

OSTERMANN: Forgive me for interrupting you, but there is something I do not understand. You claim not to have been shocked when you came into the camp. But you told me that you never had heard about any camp except Dachau. You should have been quite shocked at the sight of Auschwitz.

MÜNCH: Of course I was shocked. But compared to Delmotte I coped much better. Perhaps because as a physician the situation somehow interested me. I probably thought, this is something one must explain rationally. And so I approached the situation purely rationally and told myself, perhaps these people who have been so numbed through starvation and deprivation, they do not suffer under these cruelties as much as people in full power of their faculties would. These are thoughts I must mention, when people ask me how did I cope with the sights.

OSTERMANN: Are you trying to tell me, that you had the feeling that human beings who are so totally debilitated physically, had a deathwish?

MÜNCH: I wouldn't call it deathwish, but I do believe that the condition of being a Muselmann helped the prisoner to cope better with that whole misery than if they would have been in good physical condition. In the short run, while I was in Polish captivity, when we were ferried here and there in transports, I experienced this myself. I am not sure whether what I describe to you here was based on the experiences from the camp or whether my own experiences with such a situation played a part in it. In any case, I believe that this observation was actually true, but you probably know much more about that than I do.

OSTERMANN: Let me interrupt you here. I can assure you, that even the most demoralized Muselmann, suffering from starvation and disease, still hoped to survive. Because as long as there is breath in a person, and even the Muselmann still breathed, he still had hopes to survive, even if a miracle would have to happen. I really do not believe that the Nazis did these people a favor by sending them to the gas. The Muselmann had the same desire to survive as did the prisoner who was in better condition.

MÜNCH: No, I fear you misunderstand me. I mean to say that the Muselmann will retain hope better than the prisoner in good physical condition who still has his critical faculties. A man who is completely debilitated—as I myself experienced it—has a much better chance for hope. Perhaps that is a protective reaction, I don't know. But that is my view, my rational conclusion. But we are talking generalities again. You wanted to hear of my personal experiences.

OSTERMANN: Yes. Let us talk a moment of the most dreadful period of Auschwitz, the Hungarian transports. When the chimneys belched smoke day and night, and the workers in the crematoria could not catch up with the amount of corpses to be burned. The gassing went quicker than the cremation. There was not merely smoke, there were flames blazing into the sky because they never stopped burning. How did that strike you? What did you think at that time? These were normal, healthy people. There was a certain quota to be filled, and very few were taken into the camp. The majority of them were destined for the crematorium. And you saw all of that? What was your attitude then to such virtual mass exterminations?

MÜNCH: I had observed selections from afar by this point in time. I did not go to see them close up. You can well imagine that I did not feel any need for that. But I could not help but seeing it to get an idea of the process. I saw how they did it and I saw—if one can talk at all of a sense of humanity in this connection—that they seemed to try to do it so that the people would not realize immediately what awaited them. But then came the Hungarian transports. And with the Hungarian transports, just when they started, I was faced with the problem of being assigned to the ramp. That was my first time at the ramp, and I saw how they handled the Hungarian transports, and I had only one thought, "You've got to get out of this; you can't have a part in this." Everything else was drowned out by deliberations, such as, how can I deal with his matter so as not to get involved with it? And at that, point emotions lost their importance. My own anguish became of uppermost importance. Add to that the repeated conversations one had to listen to. Like you said, they could not keep up with the burning. I witnessed a scene there, with—what was his name—Moll . . .

OSTERMANN: Yes . . .

MÜNCH: He had been stationed in Treblinka or one of these camps. I saw Moll being consulted as expert, in order to see that everything went according to plans. They were all beginners there who had no experience, how to stack the pyres with the bodies and how to do all of that expertly so that they would burn well.

OSTERMANN: *That* had happened before . . .

MÜNCH: Perhaps it did; I did not see it. But they must have done it without any experience. And Moll was there. And when I saw how they consulted and treated the matter as if they were talking about some installations at a construction site or some such thing—that shocked me deeply. But it did not oppress me anymore rationally, because I told myself, "Well all right, that is just one step further they were forced to undertake due to the quandary they were in. They simply could not come to grips with the situation. And so they deal

with it now efficiently like they deal efficiently with all their horrors—
I mean, affairs.

OSTERMANN: You don't have to avoid the word horrors—that's what
they were.

MÜNCH: Yes, but that is only a word, nothing is really described with
that word. Maybe other languages have better words for it. But I don't
think one can describe this with words at all.

OSTERMANN: And at that point you never did have a thought about
perhaps getting out of there? It was already summer 1944; the Russian
front was approaching rapidly. Did it not occur to you to think, "Perhaps now I could manage to get away from here?"

MÜNCH: But I told you that I had promised these women . . .

OSTERMANN: Did you really believe that you could save them in spite of
the mass exterminations that went on that summer?

MÜNCH: But of course. I was not the only one who believed that.

OSTERMANN: At this point it was a matter of mass extermination of all
Jews without exception?

MÜNCH: On the contrary, our hope increased. The worse things looked
at the front, the greater the chances. I don't believe anyone dared to
say that in Auschwitz in so many words, but you could feel it in the
air. "If it comes to the point that we have to stop the gassings here,
then anyone still usable will be sent to the mines to produce V2's"
[ballistic rockets, first used in October 1942]. That was the one thing
with which they tried to hold things together, that they made a big to-
do about, how far they had advanced with these rockets. There were
miraculous stories about them, how they functioned and how the main
thing was to finish them as soon as possible. My boss, Weber, who was
always away somewhere, would talk about it when he was there. He
would say, "There is an enormous amount of work done on these
things. They are working on a gigantic scale." These were things you
probably did not know much about, you probably had a very different
outlook on the situation.

OSTERMANN: But we did. All these rumors drifted into the camp. There
were some resistance groups . . .

MÜNCH: But I bet you could only view the situation from the viewpoint of "things look bad; we are all going to the gas."

OSTERMANN: Partly yes, partly, of course, we hoped that the front would advance fast enough so that they would not be able to do that. As long as you live and breathe, you hope.

MÜNCH: That's right, quite.

OSTERMANN: I have another question. Did you really believe that they would succeed in putting this miracle weapon into action and that this war could still be won after all?

MÜNCH: No, No. I really do not remember anymore today, what I believed. I really can't say. I knew that there was something going on in that direction. But I had no idea about any atomic bombs or such things being worked on, believe me. But from the things Weber talked about, I had a clear impression that there were plans for some weapons that were not fired from canons, but which would destroy an enemy at long range or, at least, prevent deeper enemy penetration. Everyone talked very upbeat about that, and what I really thought about it, I don't remember, because the time came very soon, when everyone only thought about his own fate.

OSTERMANN: Did you see it as a ray of hope that these weapons would be put into action? Did you see any aspect at all of this whole matter, of what happened there, gruesome horrible things by your own words, that there could be any useful result from this?

MÜNCH: I did not wish for success, for an outcome of the war in favor of Hitler . . . I certainly was not of that opinion, because it was clear to me what the result would be. But I was sure that they would send as much of the labor force as was left to Germany, i.e., to the West.

OSTERMANN: But there is a clear contradiction there. In that case, they would not have had to send thousands to the gas. Most of the people in the Hungarian transports were well-nourished, able-bodied people; that is an absurd paradox. On the one hand, they thought that people must be kept well so that they could be used in the Altreich [original German area] or somewhere else in the Reich [all German occupied areas]. On the other hand, they would gas healthy, strong people in full power of their physical faculties and never even tried to take the healthier people out of all these masses in the camp to work in Germany or German-occupied areas. Something is not quite clear here.

MÜNCH: As far as I know, they selected only the weak and sick ones for the gas.

OSTERMANN: Only rarely did they do that, very rarely.

MÜNCH: Then I had been falsely informed. As I said, I only watched once, and I could not infer that much from that one time . . .

OSTERMANN: I am talking of the Hungarian transports, specifically.

MÜNCH: I was convinced that the reason for the selections was to avoid having to burn too many. There was just not enough gas. One man from the Hygiene Institute—we also had a shortage of personnel—took a truck to the Testa [Tesch & Stabenow, International Pest Control Enterprise] to fetch gas from there. The hospital orderlies of Dr. Wirth were also short of help and overtaxed and so they took two of our people, mainly to be sure that they would know to bring the right gas, that they would not bring the one with the warning marker that also was available in Auschwitz from the so-called delousing stations. They used Zyklon-B there as well, only that Zyklon had the warning marker. To fetch the gas without the marker was a big undertaking. I don't remember anymore whether we used one or two trucks. We always did have difficulties with those gas transports, from Frankfurt, or wherever they came from.

OSTERMANN: Tell me, did you not try—when you saw what was happening there and when you really had decided to protect the prisoners in your commando—to get them into the Reich in time, so that you and they could continue the research there? That would have been another possibility to get away from Auschwitz.

MÜNCH: Of course I tried that. But there was not a chance for that. That would have been wishful thinking, so to speak. They held us on a tight leash with that commando. They had noticed that our prisoners were treated better . . . In Caesar's camp they had to put up with that. In our case, they also could not say much, because we could say that we could not use undernourished people for specialized tasks. We took care of supplemental food rations for our commando and that of course annoyed them to no end because the commando marched into the camp every night [meaning they were visibly better nourished than the regular camp inmates and did not rely on the meager rations].

OSTERMANN: Well, yes, but there you had a well-trained work force. Could you not have found a reason to say, "Under these circumstances I cannot work with my commando . . . ?"

MÜNCH: No, that would never work . . .

OSTERMANN: "Send us into the Reich, and we can continue with our work there."

MÜNCH: No, that would not work because we were there for the camp, and the camp still existed, ergo, we had to be there. We did not have a general function, or at least only to a minor extent. We were specifically in charge of the bacteriological, hygienic, and other chemical examinations for the camp. At that point there were approximately 140,000 prisoners in the camp. There were a lot of places where we were needed. And they found out that things worked better with a bacteriological examining staff than with the improvised methods with only selections. During the last few months, the hospitals and infirmaries were much better furnished than they had been before.

OSTERMANN: Only the so-called Aryan infirmaries, not the Jewish ones. They were usually separate.

MÜNCH: By that time, the Aryan area was not very big anymore. The Gypsies had been gassed already. Now, that was another of the terrible events, the Gypsy camp. We had to examine the cases of Noma there. I had never even heard of that. In the textbooks it is only mentioned in footnotes, stating that this disease exists. So I said, "I have to see that." And I went to the Gypsy camp and took a look. Well you should have seen the children; they let them have the children there. But the Gypsies let the children starve and die, and the adults stuffed themselves full. That was incomprehensible and shocking to me. And if today I see gypsies, so romantic and picturesque, playing their music and all that . . . you probably heard them play their music, when they had their Sunday concerts, with their violins made of crates, touching your heart. But they let their children starve. They got their rations as family groups, and the younger the children, the less of the food they would be allotted by the older people. That was heartrending to see.

And after having experienced so many negative aspects of the so-called beautiful human soul, sights like the Gypsy camp really made you doubt humanity.

OSTERMANN: Did you ever have anything to do with the children's block in Auschwitz? There was a children's block.

MÜNCH: You mean Mengele's children's block?

OSTERMANN: No, not Mengele's, but just a children's block.

MÜNCH: I did not know that.

OSTERMANN: There were infants there. There was that baby of the woman who had given birth to it in the camp.

MÜNCH: No, I did not see that one.

OSTERMANN: You only knew Mengele's?

MÜNCH: I did not really know that one either. I really wanted to know what Mengele was doing because I was in close contact with him, and we had these political or, rather, ideological discussions. For that reason, I wanted to know what he actually did. Everyone was saying that Mengele was doing certain experimentations. So he said, "What do you think I am doing? Just normal anthropological tests like any anthropological institute does." And I said, "What kind are those? Concretely what are these experiments?" "You don't understand that," he said, and did not disclose anything more. I later tried to find out from the existing literature about him or from people who had known him what he really had been doing. No one could tell me.

OSTERMANN: But you must have known already then that he was doing twin research and that he experimented with exposure to subfreezing temperatures . . .

MÜNCH: No, I am sure he did no freezing experiments.

OSTERMANN: But these deep freeze experiments were done in the camp.

MÜNCH: I know they were done. I also know who did them. Schuhmacher and . . . [see register information: Dr. Horst Schumann. Name wrongly reported by Münch]

OSTERMANN: . . . as well as the phenol injections, etc. . . . .

MÜNCH: Exactly. And that was all.

OSTERMANN: Did that not concern you as a physician, when you found out that experiments were done on living persons, practically vivisections, scientifically speaking? Research on twins was not all he did. He tried to change the eye color of the twins and such things.

MÜNCH: No. I don't think that was done. I did not directly ask him if he changed eye colors on the twins. I only found out about that after the war. But medically speaking, that is irrelevant and insane; those are just stories. You can search wherever you want to. You will not find one concrete example of what Mengele actually did. Yes, it has been proven that he sent twins with whom he was finished experimenting into the gas, that he discussed coolly and factually, "Well, of course, if we did not need them anymore, they went into the gas like the rest."

OSTERMANN: There are depositions about his activities. There was a prisoner-doctor by the name of Ella Lingens, who worked in the prison hospital.

MÜNCH: Right. And she had nothing concrete to say . . .

OSTERMANN: No, no, there are quite concrete . . .

MÜNCH: Look, during the many trials where I was a witness, I always asked the prosecution, "How about Mengele? What did he actually do? What proofs have you against him?" "We have nothing." was the answer. And now let me tell you something. Not long ago, an old man, who seemed to have pangs of remorse, came to me from the institute in Munich where he had worked and wanted to know what Mengele had actually done. He had read in a paper that Mengele had sent the slide preparations of specimens that he had made from his twin research to the institute where the old man had worked. He claimed to have known Mengele, to have worked with him at that institute before the war. He could not believe that Mengele could have done anything criminal there.

OSTERMANN: But please . . .

MÜNCH: Just a minute. That is what he said. And I told him, "I am sorry, I can't help you, if you can't tell me what kind of specimens he sent to you . . . And he said, "Yes, he did send specimens, totally normal specimens." It is a fact that these specimens came from people Mengele had killed before preparing the specimens. But that he should have made experiments where he attempted to change hereditary features on human beings and inflicting on them pains . . . that is medically insane, no one can be so stupid. And that is why I need to know, what he had done there. . . .

OSTERMANN: Can we come back to you, if possible?

MÜNCH: I would say he did a lot of things that were crimes, for example, the examinations that he did in the crematorium. A Hungarian pathologist [Dr. Nyiszli] whom he used there documented that precisely. If he found victims with diseases that interested him, he killed them by injection and dissected them in the crematorium, that is, he had them dissected. Mostly he did not even do it himself. And those specimens he sent to the institute.

OSTERMANN: We are off the topic again. We are talking not about you but about Mengele again.

MÜNCH: If I would have to condense how I coped with Auschwitz emotionally, I would have to say that the time there, the rough times of Auschwitz—strange as it might sound—were easier to bear than the times immediately after the war's end. Actually, that is rather easily explained. If you find yourself in an extreme situation where you are forced to act and make decisions, then you can cope with the situation much better than when the pressure is off, and everything is in the past.

When I remember the time in the Polish captivity or before that, as a so-called prisoner-of-war of the Americans . . . , I wasn't sure at all what I should do at that time. Do you report to the authorities? Do you go there and say, "I was with the SS; I was in Auschwitz?" All my fellow prisoners implored me, "For God's sake, not yet. You have to let as much time pass as possible before you put yourself in front of a court or are dragged to one. Right now it will be terrible. Not only the ex-prisoners, but anyone who has suffered under Hitler will be ready to massacre anyone who ever had anything to do with the SS. That is a foregone conclusion." So there you had already a tremendous emotional tension.

When I finally ended up in a Polish prison, things really got bad—to be confined in a very small space, in a narrow cell with many Auschwitz guards and leaders. For example, the entire administration was in my cell at times and a few from the Political Department. And all of them loudly proclaimed their innocence and discussed it: "What proof have they got against me? I was only an administrator," or "I only did my soldierly duty." You know all these phrases. And there I sat in a corner and thought to myself, "I don't really belong to these people, and nevertheless, I was right in the middle of them. And above all, what are the Poles going to do to me? After what the Americans threatened to do to me, I can pretty much count on the rope." We suffered some severely emotional stresses. And the stress increased exponentially when all of them were taken for interrogations, and all of them came back very relaxed, saying, "It does not look too bad for me. They did not really want to know much." These people did not realize that the interrogators knew everything already, and that really disappointed me in my fellow prisoners, because I knew who they were and what everyone of them had done.

When it was finally my turn for my first hearing, the examining magistrate informed me immediately that I did not have to worry about any threats to my life or any punishment. There were no incriminating circumstances against me in their files. He even gave me a chance to write a letter to my wife. He said he could not mail it, but he had to go to Nuremberg, and he would get in touch with my wife and ask her to come to Nuremberg. He would tell her about me, and how I was, and that I did not have to worry about prosecution. That was such a weight off my shoulders, such an incredible experience; I cannot even describe it. All of a sudden I was told that what I had done in Auschwitz was acknowledged as innocent by those who really knew the facts about the camp. Well, it took quite a while, of course, for the judicial process to take its course.

The German authorities also exonerated me. The representative of the political prisoners group in Munich at the time, Phillip Auerbach, whom I had known in Auschwitz, not only encouraged me greatly, but he also did everything he could to help me get a job. That really made me feel good. And after that, there was a long time when I desperately—not really desperately, but purposefully—tried to forget everything that had happened. But, of course, situations evoking memories repeatedly rose from the past. That was a hard time, until

I worked through that, and I was finally forced to admit to myself, "Sure, Auschwitz, as we now know, was probably mankind's worst realization of atrocities, of inhumanities. But how did humanity cope with such situations in earlier times?" This was the reason that I began to research seriously, as much as my time allowed, the historically extraordinary times in which genocide and war-time brutalities occurred. That research evoked varied emotional reactions in me, and the emotional impressions of the Auschwitz reality rearranged themselves in my mind's eye. I can't go into detail about these thoughts and events because I have not quite sorted them out for myself. I have flirted with the idea to write something of my feelings in book form. But I am afraid I do not have the talent or the words. One would have to express all of one's emotions in such an undertaking, and that I cannot do talking about all this. I just recall that I have never asked any prisoner, when talking to one of them, how he could cope with his fate in Auschwitz. I don't want to say his actual experiences, but the difficulty of dealing with the experience. As I saw it, the prisoners' situation was so self-evident that there could not be a great variety of views concerning that. How did you handle it? I would really like to know.

ADJUSTING FOR SURVIVAL

OSTERMANN: In order to explain that to you I will have to narrate a few key experiences, because they played a large part in clarifying my attitude vis-à-vis the SS or how I coped with the experience later. I already mentioned how I came to Birkenau, and that, due to the fact that I was not on the list, I was lucky enough to be assigned to the Political Department. As I said, I was not housed in Auschwitz I, but had to walk daily between Birkenau and Auschwitz I. These were difficult conditions, and by being in Birkenau I saw all the things that happened there. I don't know whether you knew that Birkenau had a lot of groundwater; it was a marshy area.

MÜNCH: I knew that.

OSTERMANN: If it rained for not more than half an hour, you sank into the mud up to your knees. One day, for example, I witnessed the following after the roll call: the so-called Muselmen [women]—these horrible, starved, and sick stick figures—would frequently fall down into the mud and did not have the strength to get up out of it. They stayed there and became almost invisible in the mud. You could hardly recognize them as human beings. And there were rats in Birkenau; never in my life have I seen rats of that size. And the rats would nibble on these mud encrusted corpses. Sometimes they were not quite dead yet. The corpse commandos would collect the corpses. Many times they would only find these mud, clay, and filth encrusted corpses when they would look where the rats sat and what they were nibbling on. What the rats had left they would collect. Aside from the heap of corpses that I mentioned to you as my very first impression standing by block 25, this was my second extremely drastic experience in Birkenau.

MÜNCH: May I interrupt you with a question? These corpse commandos, did they consist of women from Birkenau?

OSTERMANN: Of course they were women, women prisoners from the camp. That was a work commando like many others, a so-called Aussenkommando. They probably received somewhat bigger food rations because they had to carry all these bodies, though the corpse commandos had wheelbarrows. They would pile the bodies in front of block 25. Another significant experience was the following: after the roll call, before marching out to work, we saw two or three women hanging on the electric fence. They probably went to the fence out of desperation because they simply could not cope with the circumstances they found themselves in. The moment that someone came close to the electric fence, the guards in the guard towers would shoot at them. Because touching the fence would somehow short circuit the current, and they wanted to avoid that, they would shoot first. You see, these were key experiences of my very first days there, and they affected me frightfully, because I am by nature a very compassionate person. I probably had more compassion with my fellow prisoners in camp than with myself, if I remember correctly. I could not stand the suffering of these human beings; that touched me much deeper than my own fate. But that is probably an innate trait with me, and that is why I never became numbed to the suffering and never stopped feeling compassionate about the women around me. Then came the time when I did not have to walk back and forth between Birkenau and the Stabsgebäude but was housed there. That was a building where the SS women lived upstairs, and we had dormitories in the basement. That arrangement was not prompted by humanitarian considerations but merely because we were in direct daily contact with the SS, and they wanted to protect themselves from the many diseases of the camp by isolating us from other prisoners. There is one thing I would add concerning my Birkenau experiences. According to you, the SS only beat when there was need for punishment for some reason. I have to deny that categorically, because I saw myself how many poor, totally broken, starved, skeleton-like women were bludgeoned and beaten for no reason whatsoever. The SS would use the whips they had stuck into their boots for these beatings. On that score the SS women distinguished themselves. They sometimes behaved worse and more beastly than the men. We know that women, if they are cruel, are many times more cruel than men. These were my first impressions of Birkenau. How was life in the Political Section? Let me explain; there was a subdivision called the registry office. It was located in a barrack next to the old, small crematorium [crematorium I] diagonally across from the actual Political Section and consisted of two offices; one office was the Political Section, and one was the registry. Our immediate superior was SS-Oberscharführer Kirschner. It was, of course, not a registry where marriages were celebrated, rather, our activities consisted of writing death certificates, day in, day out. That is how I acquired my knowledge of all the physicians' names in Auschwitz who always had to sign these death certificates. And as cause of death there were more or less the same diseases listed over and over again: edema, myocarditis, and meningitis, etc. The actual causes of death, such as spotted fever or typhus, rarely, if ever, appeared on the death certificates. They probably did not want the outside world to know about these epidemic diseases because the certificates were sent to the bereaved families. There were also small rooms in the barrack. They were used for interrogations by the SS of the Political Section. These were either interrogations of prisoners from the camp who had transgressed against one of the camp rules, or of

Polish families who had been arrested because someone in their families had been caught distributing leaflets, or engaging in sabotage or partisan activities. That is what they called "Sippenhaft" [kinship arrest]. In the corridor of the barrack, you could sometimes see whole families from grandfather to grandchild waiting to be interrogated.

And now I come to the heart of the matter. Aside from the fact that we wrote death certificates from morning to night, in my office, at least, we were also used by the SS to record the interrogations. We were brought in to type the interrogation as it was conducted. Sometimes we did it after the questioning; sometimes during the questioning, that depended on the degree of interrogation. And rarely was the atmosphere lenient; beating, yelling, and kicking were the normal treatment of the prisoners. For us, as prisoners, this was hard to take. But the worst room in the barrack was the room for the severe interrogations. In that room was the swing, I don't know if you are familiar with the term "swing" in Auschwitz. That was a structure like a trestle with a bar across—it was called the Bogner swing since it was the invention of Oberscharführer Bogner. Human beings were hung there, tied hand and foot and hung there like a pig. And then they would be turned. And every time that the buttocks would turn to the top, they would be beaten mercilessly. The people would be beaten until they would confess to anything at all or until they fainted. Then they poured water over them; sometimes they would give them Apolinaris mineral water—normally reserved for the SS—and then the questioning would continue. You could hear the screams throughout the whole barrack, and of course the people waiting their turn outside would hear them too. What do I want to imply with that? You said that you had very good relations to your prisoners. Well, I can tell you, our relations with the SS with whom we worked every day was not bad either. You cannot expect an SS man to yell at and beat a prisoner with whom he is together practically from morning 'till night. The prisoner assigned to him usually was his right hand, and he needed her. I must add here that they would switch secretaries, assign them to a different SS man so that no possible fraternization could occur. That was one of their safety measures. But for me, that an SS man could be a decent human

being just because he was nice to me, that was out of the question; there was an SS-man to whom I was frequently assigned, Unterscharführer Hoyer; he was very nice to me and even shared some things from a food parcel he had received, but he would beat prisoners within an inch of their lives. With all his friendliness, that was not a decent human being in my view. Take the secretary who worked for Lachmann; she cannot describe him as a good person just because he said a few kind words to her after he had been in the old crematorium for some executions. One has to differentiate. I want to tell you now about one of my very strong, key experiences. I had mentioned that according to the Nuremberg laws I was a mixed breed. That is a half Jew with a Christian mother. One fine day my mother decided to get on the train and come to Auschwitz without obtaining permission or anything.

MÜNCH: How did your mother know you were in Auschwitz?

OSTERMANN: I was just going to explain that. First of all, my relatives were informed that I had been assigned to a "protective custody" camp, namely Ravensbrück, after I had been dismissed from the Gestapo prison. They then inquired at Ravensbrück and found out that I was in Auschwitz. Since I had these Aryan relatives, I was allowed to write a ten-line letter once a month.

MÜNCH: I did not know that such things existed.

OSTERMANN: Yes, the so-called Aryan prisoners, or those who had Christian families, were allowed to receive parcels—they did not always get them—and could write a censured letter once a month, i.e., The usual "I am well" and so on. And in one of these letters, to reassure my mother, I mentioned, "I work in an office in the Political Section. Don't worry about me." I managed to insert the word "Political Section" in an innocuous letter. Now that is important for the rest of my story; remember it. One fine day I am called to the office of Oberscharführer Kirschner, who, as I mentioned, worked in the main Political Section diagonally across from the barrack. He said to me, "Your mother was here. But she had no visitor's permit, and of course she could not see you. But I told her to go to Berlin and get a visitor's permit, and then she can see you. She left a parcel for you." I was dumbfounded. My mother must have been insane. One does not even go near a camp voluntarily. And it was not clear to me how the whole thing happened: how did she get into the camp in the first place. There was, after all, the major guard post chain and the small guard post chain before one came to the camp area at all. Five weeks later I am called to Kirschner's office again. Kirschner was only interim head of the department, Untersturmführer Grabner had been removed, and Schurz followed him. As I said, I had to cross the street to the main building, and he stands in the door, the entrance door to the building. And while I crossed the street, I remembered there was a light drizzle, he motions with his thumb, and I follow the direction of his thumb and see my mother go towards the exit. She had just reached the wire fence where the guard stood and, of course, in this moment I did not think whether it was permitted or not, I just called: "Mama." She turns around and starts to come toward me, and I motioned her away and I only called out to her: "Mama, don't ever come to Auschwitz again, never never." And she went to the gate, crying.

Only much later did I find out how all this happened. At her first visit, she simply went up to the guard on duty and said: "I want to go to the Political Section." When she said that word unhesitatingly, the guard, of course, thought she knew her way around, and he said, "Well, you know that is right there." Then she stood in the corridor there and did not know where to go. An Unterscharführer by the name of Schmidt came by and said, "What can I do for you?" My mother was well dressed and impressive, and she said: "I would like to speak to your superior," and he answered "I am sorry. My superior, Untersturmführer Grabner, is not here at the moment, but you can see his second in command, Unterscharführer Kirschner." "All right," she said, "then take me to him." And my mother went into Kirschner's room, and he said, "What can I do for you, madam?" And she said, "I would like to speak to my daughter." And he said, "To which SS unit does she belong?" And my mother said, "She does not belong to any SS unit; she is a prisoner here." "Well then, you must know in which commando she works." And she answered, "My daughter works in your office." Well, he knew that only prisoners with the Jewish star worked in his commando—the Christian Poles who worked there were actually also destined for the Final Solution, because it was planned to gas us all if we were not needed anymore, because we were bearers of secrets. He looked at her totally perplexed and said, "But that is not possible." He called his secretary and asked her, "Is there a certain so-and-so working in our commando?" And she answered, "Of course, she works in the registry office." So he dismissed her and just stared at my mother.

Then my mother told him her story—that she was a Christian married to a Jew, that her whole family had been Nazis, when it was still illegal to be one, and that she had been quasi the black sheep of the family. And because I had been a member of the Jewish community on the day the Nuremberg laws became effective, I had to wear the star, and that was the reason I had been sent to the camp. They kept talking, and it evolved that this Kirschner was also from Dresden, just like my mother. That was when he gave her the tip to try to go to Berlin and obtain a visitor's permit. Of course, she never got that permit at the Reich Security office. They reviled her roundly. "Jewish whore" was one of the milder insults, but luckily they did not keep her there. And again she made her way back to Auschwitz without a permit. Kirschner took pity on her and let her see me from afar, but of course she could not talk to me. And he promised my mother at that time that he would keep an eye on me.

But now I have to tell you how, even though an SS man holds his hand over you, you can come into a situation where they drop you like a hot potato. I had let myself be persuaded by another prisoner, a secretary of Liebehenschel's, to send an illegal letter through her. That prisoner had a lot of opportunities to talk to members of the SS, and among others, she became acquainted with an SS matron, with whom she started to have longer conversations. It was already April '44 and, some uncertainty was in the air. The matron must have thought, "A bit of fraternization with a prisoner might not be out of place; perhaps she can help me one day." So she told the secretary, "Listen, you can write to your family through me." I really did not feel very secure doing it but did not want to be a coward. I wanted to prove how daring I was, and so I sent the letter to my mother under that SS matron's return address. My mother answered to the same address. I found out later that in her letter she asked me not to use this subterfuge. I would not write anything different in my regular letters anyway. This matron was arrested; she was accused of gold smuggling manipulations [stealing from the gold taken from the transports]—her premises were searched, and my mother's letter was found. Kirschner called me to his office and said, "There is nothing I can do for you anymore, now you must go to Birkenau." That is how I returned to Birkenau, to the delight of my immediate superior in the registry office, Unterscharführer Kristan, an East Prussian junker who somehow always had looked at me with suspicion. He did not know what to make of me. I was not a Jew, I was not a Christian. My mother came to Auschwitz. I was blonde, had blue eyes—all these things disturbed him terribly. For him, I was something of a hybrid, and to him my whole family appeared somewhat schizophrenic: on one side the ardent Nazi family, on the other the Jewish father. My mother had been divorced from him since I was three, but then had married another Jewish man, a lawyer. She was widowed in 1931, and since that time my mother and I had lived alone.

My whole life seemed to have proceeded in a somewhat schizophrenic manner. I visited my relatives on my mother's side and listened to them singing the Nazi songs and found that quite all right. As a child and even as an adolescent, I did not comprehend the political implications of that. Back in Vienna, the majority of my friends and acquaintances were Jewish: I suppose that could make me appear schizophrenic.

Unterscharführer Kristan had been so suspicious of me that he was delighted to get me out of his sight and volunteered to personally escort me on foot to Birkenau. And all during that walk he kept saying, "I always told you that you would end up where all the others end up." He already had said frequently to me, while I worked under him and had displeased him somehow, "You don't have to be so smug around here; you'll end up where all the others end up." These were his favorite remarks to me. He really felt that he had achieved great satisfaction by bringing me to Birkenau personally. Thus I arrived in Birkenau and was received by the head matron, Hasse, with roaring insults. Then I was interrogated again. They wanted to know if I had known the matron who had offered the cover address, and I said, "No, I did not know her. I received the address from someone else." That was true, but even if I had known her name I would not have denounced her; that is not my habit. So, of course, they wanted the name of the person I had the address from, and I said, "Please let us not go into that." And she said, "You really don't have to tell us that; we know the name anyway, because there was also a letter from your buddy." That was true; two days later, she was also in Birkenau. I was assigned to the penal commando, a separate block, received a Flucht Punkt ["escape spot," consisting of the letters IL for "Im Lager" (in camp) in black cloth on the back of the clothing with a red cloth spot approximately 3–4' in diameter], which meant that I was not allowed to leave the camp area. That was actually an advantage for me, because they could not send me to work in an outside commando. I had to work within the camp. I had to shovel sand from one side of a sandpile to the other side, a rather unproductive labor; we used to call it "moving mountains."

My workplace was not near the penal block, but in the quarantine camp. There we were to help break in the new arrivals, who at that time arrived in ever decreasing numbers. The Hungarian transports had not started yet, and the normal transports had decreased: just a few transports from Germany and one from Holland [probably spring 1944]. In the evening we would return to the penal block. I was the only one with a Jewish star in there. All the others were mainly asocials, i.e., prostitutes who had been caught organizing or having lesbian relationships.

I don't want to go into detail about the lesbian relations. But in the penal block I came in contact with such elements for the first time. There were big Fritz and little Fritz and big Karl and little Karl: that's how the women called each other to distinguish who played the man and who the woman. It was a strange world for me, but it did not affect me.

A very deeply felt experience was Mala Zimmetbaum's death. She was a Polish Jewess who had arrived with a Belgian transport. She had a rather privileged position as interpreter in the hospital block and through her work could maintain contact with male prisoners. A love affair developed between her and a Polish prisoner, and the two of them escaped, of course with outside help. At that time, the Hungarian transports were already arriving. I did not know much about these transports at the time. Later I saw the statistics about them. There were in that period twenty thousand gassings a day. Some historians doubt these statistics. They dug ditches where they threw the dead in to burn them. They could keep pace with the gassing but not with the cremations. I can only relate that second hand, because I was not there; but I was told that they would throw half-dead babies into the fire.

MÜNCH: I had heard that also from our side. There was a scandal about it; that is how I know.

OSTERMANN: In late summer, they removed my escape spot, and I was sent on an outside commando. In the vicinity of Birkenau, there were a number of carp ponds, but by now they were dried out, and we were supposed to level them out. That was very hard work. One day we returned from work to the camp, and we saw that everyone was standing on the parade ground. We were told everyone had to stop at the parade ground; we could not disperse. We saw a gallows had been raised in the middle of the ground. At the time Mala had escaped, we had to stand for hours in roll call. We were told we would stand in formation until Mala had been found. That obviously became impossible, because Mala was not caught for five or six days. Whether she was betrayed or caught by coincidence, I don't know. [tr. note: Mala got sick, and it seems the doctor who was called denounced them].

Both were caught, the Pole and the girl. And as we marched in from the outside, the parade ground was filled, and the word spread like wildfire through the ranks: Mala had been caught and they had the gallows ready to hang her in public. And there she stood under the gallows with some Rapportführer. I don't remember his name anymore, but he was especially known for his cruelty. He stood in front of her, and at that moment she tried to cut her wrists with a razorblade. She probably preferred dying by bleeding to death over hanging. He pulled her arm back, and she, almost like a reflex, drew back, hit him in the face in front of the whole assembled camp and screamed, "I know I'll have to die, but you, pig, are going to croak in a much worse way than I." She was not hanged, but they brought a wheelbarrow and having lost lots of blood already, they loaded her into it, and escorted by that SS man, she was taken to the gas chamber. They purposely tried to prolong her suffering. "The gallows is too good for you," they told her. The Polish male prisoner was hung in the men's camp. That was one of my many experiences in Auschwitz.

Another experience occurred later, when there were less transports, and the Russian front came closer and closer. You know there was the Sonderkommando, the commando consisting of only Jewish male prisoners who had to lead the other prisoners to the gas chamber. They would usually be rotated after a few months and sent to the gas. During their work span, they did have better food. They really had a bad time of it. Many times they had to lead their own mother, or brother or a neighbor, a relative or a sister to the gas and take the corpses from the gas chamber to the crematorium. And when it became known that the gassing would stop in the near future, because there were no more transports arriving, they knew very well that their turn had come. They organized an uprising. Through some underground passages, they managed to obtain guns and ammunition. Actually, the ammunition was not obtained underground at all. Girls who worked in the Union [an ammunition factory in Auschwitz III, the factory area] and who handled gunpowder, smuggled small quantities of it out of the factory. These four girls—all Polish Jewesses—were publicly hanged in Auschwitz on January 6, 1945.

MÜNCH: Which four?

OSTERMANN: The four girls from the Union factory who had smuggled the gunpowder out. To get back to the story, we were inside the camp, and suddenly we heard heavy gunfire. We all threw ourselves flat on the ground. That was the revolt of the Sonderkommando, October 7, 1944, who probably thought to themselves, "we will not be able to liberate ourselves, but if we have to get killed we shall take a few SS with us." That is what happened. None of them of course survived, but a few SS died too. That was also a key experience in that period. After the revolt, the SS were of course not exactly friendly to us. There would be beatings without cause. The SS matrons behaved in such a manner that one asked oneself whether these were women, who were mothers, who might bear children. But in spite of everything that I suffered, my compassion always remained my determining way of life.

In 1942, when I was still in Birkenau, walking into Auschwitz every morning I met a girl on the camp street who worked in the Kanada commando. That was the time when the Jewish blocks were still treated especially vicious. At that time I already lived in the wooden barrack as an administrative prisoner. When we met she said, "You know, we did not get any bread again in the Jewish block. Would you trade my margarine ration for your bread ration?" And I told her, "Keep your margarine; I will give you half of my bread ration." For me it was nothing out of the ordinary to help my fellow inmates. I always managed to replace what I gave away from some other source. That girl later on worked in the SS blockleader office in Auschwitz I, where she met her future husband, the Lagerälteste of Auschwitz I, Dr. Dürrmayer. When she came to Auschwitz I she waved to me as we stood in the roll call. We stood roll call in a narrow corridor in the basement of the Stabsgebäude. I did not recognize her, and she approached me and said, "Have you forgotten? You gave me your bread one day on the camp street." Things like that had always been a matter of course for me. That habit I maintained even in camp.

One day, while I was in the penal commando, the order came for several blocks to remain standing outside after roll call. A transport was being put together. That was my first acquaintance with a cattle car; I went on transport.

MÜNCH: When was that?

OSTERMANN: November 1, 1944. That is to say I was in Birkenau in the penal commando from April until November '44.

MÜNCH: I am beginning to count the time elapsed for you in Birkenau. You must have been close to being a Muselmann.

OSTERMANN: No—thank God—I was not. By that time I was already an old hand at Auschwitz. You could recognize it on my prisoner number, 21946, that I was a prisoner since 1942. My tattoo was without a triangle and without either an *A* or a *B* preceding the number. The numbers after 100,000 began with *A* and then with *B*, and they were done in a smaller tattoo. And due to that fact, an old inmate would already know one or the other Blockälteste who would slip you a little something. Or one had access to the kitchen on the sly; one knew one's way around. If I had been dependent on the camp food, I probably would have been a Muselmann after that length of time. But that does not mean that I did not pass my Muselmann time. I did that before I came to the Political Section in Auschwitz. I had spotted fever and typhoid fever and malaria. Only I was very lucky; I had very light cases of these diseases. I had the malarial chills and the bouts of fever only sporadically. Only after the war, by taking a bloodtest, was it determined that I had had malaria.

MÜNCH: But that is unusual.

OSTERMANN: Perhaps the body was inured by these diseases. I was of course no heavyweight in 1944, but also no Muselmann, not just skin and bones.

MÜNCH: I understand. And you were sent on transport.

OSTERMANN: Yes. I was sent on transport on November 1, 1944 with a large number of people, and we were stuffed like sardines in the cattle car. We could not even sit down. They put two tin buckets in the car, probably old cucumber or marmalade containers, for elimination needs. Then the doors were locked, and this finished my Auschwitz stay. We were being transported to a new camp. I just remembered something important, however, that I want to tell you about. But for that I have to go a bit farther into the past. My father, in his second marriage, was also married to a Christian who divorced him in 1938, in spite of a daughter born to that marriage who was five years younger than I and in spite of the fact that she could have provided protection from transports and persecution for my father, being an "Aryan spouse." During the first World War, my father was a first lieutenant, had volunteered twice for front service, in spite of being 60 percent disabled, and had received, among other decorations, the gold medal with crossed swords for valor. Hitler had promised veterans like him that they would be protected since they had fought for the fatherland. The only advantage my poor father had from all that was that he was not sent to Theresienstadt before 1943. Of course, he had hoped to remain there for the duration of the war, but that did not happen. After a few months, he was already sent on transport to Auschwitz. Though my parents were divorced, my mother still looked after my father a bit. Before being deported, he had found out from her that I worked in the Political Section in Auschwitz. He was sent to the Theresienstadt Family camp in Auschwitz. In that camp families were allowed to stay together: men, women, and children, and, of course, that gave some of them hope. Father met a man in that camp who worked in a commando that supplied laundry to the Political Section, to our office. That commando also supplied all camp sections with laundry, including the Theresienstadt Family camp. He was a man with a green triangle, denoting him as a habitual criminal, but he was a very decent and friendly fellow. One day he asked one of my comrades, "Is there a Dagmar Bock working in the registry office? She is supposed to work in the Political Section." "Yes," she answered, and then she called me: "There is a guy here who wants to talk to you. He says he has a message for you." I already knew that my father was here. Because, though it was forbidden to tell the colleagues who worked in a different section about any transports, somehow we were always informed. "There is a new transport from Theresienstadt, etc." One day I was told, "Listen, there is a man on this transport list with the same last name as yours." And since they told me the first name was Oswald, I knew that was my father. So there was this prisoner, who brought me the following message: "In the Theresienstadt Family camp there is a certain Oswald Bock, and he thinks that his daughter is working here in the Political Section, and he wanted to know if I could not get him some food, a piece of bread and [my father being a heavy smoker] some tobacco or some such things." We got in touch with each other like that two or three times, but rather sporadically. Sometimes I did not hear from him for two or three weeks at a time. Then the laundry prisoner would come back; in the meantime, I had saved some things for my father, which I gave him. My father confirmed in a letter the receipt of the things, so that I should not worry that the prisoner kept the things, because he had received everything. One day, when I wanted to give the laundry prisoner a few things again, he said: "You don't have to send anything anymore. Your father isn't there anymore." Being an experienced Auschwitz inmate, I knew immediately what he was saying. Later some of my colleagues who had access to the lists of the gassed inmates confirmed it for me. Almost the entire Theresienstadt Family camp had been sent to the gas. I just want to make the point with this, that my father, in spite of his merits in the service of the fatherland, went to the gas like the rest. That was very typical of the Third Reich tendencies, that they would not keep their word even to the war veterans.

MÜNCH: This can't really be stated anymore explicitly than you state it.

OSTERMANN: If you want to talk of honor and fidelity—and that seems to be the wording in the SS emblem—this is one case where all honor and all fidelity and all promises were broken and forgotten.

MÜNCH: Since matters so personal really touch a person deeply, I can well imagine, that your situation . . .

OSTERMANN: Of course it hit me hard, even though we had no personal contact.

MÜNCH: Of course.

OSTERMANN: I would quickly like to tell you of my liberation. That also did not happen from one day to the next. I was liberated on May 2, 1945, on the road to Mecklenburg, because, as I had mentioned, I had been deported from Auschwitz to a satellite camp of Ravensbrück, Malchow. The SS dragged us around for two more days on the roads. They were not our regular SS; those had already taken off. These SS were old, Volkssturm men [overaged men, drafted into the army as a last measure of defense in 1945] dressed in SS uniforms but without the SS emblems, only with swastikas on black background. These old men marched behind us with fixed bayonets. On May 2, I was liberated by American tank forces on the road near Lübs [a town in northern Germany, in the state of Mecklenburg]. Everything there was already in the final stages of disintegration. We marched through empty villages whose people had fled ahead of the Russians. The next day, the Russians were there already. After the first liberation, we walked a bit farther, spent the night in a haystack, and woke up the next morning as free people. What we were not aware of was that the Russians had arrived during the night.

Something interesting happened while we were walking on the road. A group of cyclists rode by, former SS guards from Malchow, the satellite camp, including the camp commander, Kleinschmidt. They smiled at us and greeted us in a most friendly manner. It did not suit us very well, that they should go free and unscathed, though I can't really say that these were thoughts of pure vengeance. But that they should ride past us with a smile and a wink, that was a bit much . . . Some former inmates had to have left the marching columns, and gone ahead, because when we met the first American tank troops, the KZ inmates stood there already and the SS men as well, though they had disguised themselves in civilian clothing. The Americans must have already...

MÜNCH: ...grabbed them...

OSTERMANN: Well yes, taken them. Their shirt sleeves were torn to the top, they had immediately checked whether the men had their bloodgroup tattooed under the arm, because that was the distinctive mark of SS members. Then we were told, those who wished to stay on the American side should continue on in the direction of Hamburg, i.e., North West, and those who did not mind staying on the Russian side could stay or go back. I only wanted one thing: I wanted by all means to get to Vienna. I had not heard from my mother since we had left Auschwitz in November. My mother also had no news of me, though she had received information that I had been sent to Ravensbrück. Therefore, I only wanted to go to Vienna, Hamburg was of no interest to me. I began my retreat in the direction of my homeland.

I traveled via a destroyed Berlin, gave a speech in Herzberg an der Elster [a town in east Germany] about the concentration camp, and then continued on in the direction of Dresden. Of course, I hardly recognized Dresden. My grandmother's house had been destroyed like all the other houses. I remembered that close to her house had been a hospice [a kind of hotel run by a religious organization], and I thought perhaps I could find shelter there. On the road I had met other former inmates from the KZ, among others, a man who had been liberated in Buchenwald, and who had decided to travel with me to Vienna. He was also a Viennese like me. I found the hospice, and there in a corner stood my grandmother's husband. I was almost dumbstruck and said, "Opa [grandpa], what are you doing here?" He looked very scared and did not want to talk to me. He did not seem surprised at all, but acted as if he had just seen me yesterday. He motioned to me to be quiet. And when I asked: "Where is Oma?" He finally pointed in a sort of sign language: round the corner of the house. I began to understand his fear, because a Russian car stood in front of the house he pointed to.

I rang the doorbell of the house; my aunt looked out of the window and my grandmother too. I thought my grandmother would jump out of the window, she was in such a hurry. She could not believe that I was still alive. I did, however, not stay very long in Dresden, but continued through Czechoslovakia, freed an uncle from prison who really was not guilty of collaboration with the Hitler regime: he was a scientist, a chemist, a dreamer. Then I walked through Czechoslovakia to Vienna, and finally I stood in front of our house. The house had burned down, and for the first time in these three years, I cried bitterly. Suddenly I noticed a small piece of paper stuck to the ruin; it was my mother's address. An additional little incident happened right there, I want you to know. I was leaning against the ruined wall, and suddenly someone taps me on the shoulder and says, "Excuse me, what is that number on your arm and why are you crying?" And I say, "That is a concentration camp number." And the woman says, "Do you by any chance have a pencil and paper. I would like to write your number down. When they start again with the lotteries, I want to bet this number." That was my first [postwar] encounter with Vienna and the Viennese.

MÜNCH: That is really extraordinary. How did you cope with that?

OSTERMANN: I can describe that to you in a few words. You probably think that I harbored all kinds of vengeful feelings, which would be normal to assume. I did not have any. No vengeful feelings at all. What depressed me most were the impressions that I could not get out of my head. For the longest time, I kept dreaming of Auschwitz, had certain anxieties, and I was afraid of large gatherings of people. It is possible, however, that I was less traumatized than many others, because first of all, I was young and survived relatively healthily, and I found my mother again. That was one of the main healing aspects of the post-camp time, because my mother had always been the central figure of my life. My fervent desire to live to see her again helped me to bear the camp and survive it. It is also possible that it was basically my life affirming nature that played a large part in my survival. It was only natural that my dreams were filled with images of that horrible time, but during the day the routine of everyday life kept me occupied. I was so happy to have found my mother and to have a home; even though the old home had been destroyed, we had managed to create a new home for ourselves. All this helped me to cope emotionally with the past. Only after I became a mother myself did the old fears return somewhat, the fear of the events of the past repeating themselves and hurting my child. But as for myself, I coped well within a relatively short time. Getting older, however, brings back the memories.

THERE ARE NO MORE WORDS LEFT. . .

Here the filmmaker interjects himself into the dialogue:

DIRECTOR: Dr. Münch, what would you tell people who are today saying that the Holocaust never happened, that Auschwitz is a lie and a fraud?

MÜNCH: If someone says Auschwitz is a lie or a fraud, then I refuse to say much to that person. I say the facts are clear and obvious, and no one can doubt them, and more I do not say to such a person. Whoever clings to such issues that are being published God knows where, you well know that he is malicious and has a personal agenda, to want to cover up such facts that cannot be silenced.

DIRECTOR: Dr. Münch, what would happen if you found yourself in a similar situation today?

MÜNCH: If someone would suggest that I could be in a similar situation, I would answer him that it would be unimaginable that such an event could happen to me again. However, I am almost certain that it could happen to other people who have never heard of the Holocaust, let alone experienced it. Because looking at the world during these last fifty years, I have determined that man has not learned from the past, that his nature is destructive when he gets into a position of power, which from our vantage point today looks dangerous. It is possible that again entire nations, or at least large masses of people, could be fascinated by such power and be moved to deeds that could be compared to Auschwitz. That is the personal conclusion I draw from what I see and hear around me today.

DIRECTOR: Dr. Münch, you have repeatedly asserted that between your emotions—those things in your heart, in your gut, and your soul—

and the things that you can put into words about Auschwitz, there is a big gap. Can you possibly explain to Mrs. Ostermann what it means, not to be able to express these things?

MÜNCH: I must stress once more, I cannot express in detail what it is that makes it so hard for me to express my emotions about my Auschwitz experiences. But perhaps it might be connected to the fact that in a man, unlike a woman, the emotions of the heart are sometimes blocked by the brain, which builds a sort of cover over the emotions, and a situation might arise where one begins to doubt oneself. The older one gets, and I do find that in myself, the stronger the tendency to a transfiguration of the past seems to creep in. That tendency is built into all of us: some things become overpowered by the intellect, and when the emotions then come to the fore, they appear altered somehow. I can only talk of my own conclusion, and I simply cannot express it any more precisely. I cannot give you an unequivocal answer to this. If ever I would be in such a situation again, I, of course, would know from past experience how dangerous it is, to sweep the things one does not want to see under the cover, that is to say, if one lets repression take its course. I believe I would have been healed of such a contamination.

The impossibility of explaining Auschwitz to people who never had such an experience lies in the fact that all the books and facts and figures written about Auschwitz cannot make its true reality come alive. If someone asks me today about my views about Auschwitz, I would have to give an ambiguous answer. When I first returned from Auschwitz after the war, I preached about it with missionary zeal, because I felt that something had to be done to prevent a repetition of such events. It is possible that everyday life and being in a profession overwhelmed my priorities, and I was deflected from my zeal. Then the years passed, and I had to recognize in the back of my mind that it was questionable whether humanity could be influenced through sermons and publications. Today I have arrived at almost the opposite pole. I do things if people assure me that through my presentations I can influence some people, but, unfortunately, I am not convinced that it will have the success that I would desire.

OSTERMANN: Well, my experiences after the war in connection with my past are of course very different from Dr. Münch's. Immediately after the war, everyone was full of compassion. Everyone tried to tell me how he had helped, how he was against the regime. Today things are different. My generation is much more reserved in this respect, i.e., they avoid any confrontation with it. On the other hand, I must say that the young people with whom one comes into contact are much more affirmative in their views. They can be convinced of the importance of the past, and they are willing to work hard to prevent a repetition of the past. How I feel personally about you, you could easily deduce from our conversation. I cannot hate you, but perhaps there is a small measure of disdain for a man who, in spite of the fact that he knew better, went along with everything. But as I said, I do not hate; that is not my style. I have conducted this conversation without hate or resistance, without any intention to reproach you for all the ills of the past. I wanted to stick to the facts and was more or less curious how you coped with it all. You did try to describe it to me in some form. Much of it I can accept, but, to be honest, much of it I can't. Whether you can understand it or not, one thing is certain: I have no personal feelings of dislike or hate; only, as I mentioned before, there is a certain inner restraint, perhaps not noticeable externally, but it exists. And I am sure you understand that also.

MÜNCH: I noticed that not only in talking with you, but in my contact with all former prisoners. That is based on the nature of the thing. And I accept that fully because it can hardly be otherwise. But I tried to depict my point of view, and I hope that I clarified some things to you, that not everything fits the same mold. Just because one was a member of a criminal organization does not mean that he is automatically a criminal.

OSTERMANN: No.

MÜNCH: It matters to me, that I have hopes to have made this fact clear to you.

OSTERMANN: Well, I mean . . .

MÜNCH: My experience with many attempts to contact prisoners whom I did not know personally from the Auschwitz time have always proven to me that my fears of being misunderstood were justified. Mainly because the prisoner sees Auschwitz from a different angle. For that reason, he cannot comprehend my situation, wherein I was convinced that I had acted rightly; perhaps he can intellectually somehow, but never emotionally. There he always has misgivings. That is why I mentioned right at the beginning of our conversation that I am inhibited in talking to you. Though I do not have a bad conscience. Not merely because I was acquitted by the court, but for myself, I have no bad conscience either.

OSTERMANN: There is only one thing I can say to that: Yes you were acquitted, de jure, that is right, but de facto for me, you belonged to an organization that committed inhuman cruelties, even if you did do nothing yourself. But you served this government and this unit to the end. And that is what causes this inner "restraint" that I must have towards you, even though I understand you better from your narrative and from your fate and do not consider you a murderer or one who had a hand in doing evil. But the mere fact that you served this regime with your science and contributed to prolonging the war or contributed within the camp to the maintenance of that camp, that is part of my restraint towards you. Nothing personal, but I cannot overcome this sentiment.

MÜNCH: Of course. And in my view that is the key for the fact that among human beings there can never be complete, real understanding. As you describe it and explain it, this is exactly the first step leading to intolerance, i.e., to the impossibility of understanding the other. And if tolerance is impossible to achieve, and obviously this is the case—within the construct of human nature or European nature or however we want to call it—then this lack of understanding will remain a fact like so many other things that can not be eliminated from this world because that is how we all are.

OSTERMANN: My psychic injuries were harder to bear than my bodily misery. They were what hurt me first and foremost. I was brought up to be liberal and philanthropic, and the humiliations I experienced, the psychic injuries of being dehumanized to the level of subhuman species, that injured me deeply, emotionally. That is probably the one aspect of the camp I can never shake. Of course, to have to see how my comrades suffered and died horrible deaths was appalling, but the feeling of having been dehumanized stayed with me even more. That one can be humiliated into one's deepest, innermost core, in a manner that is indescribable, that is a psychic injury I can never overcome.

MÜNCH: To sum up, you also cannot completely give vent to your emotions verbally, as I already said during our conversation. It is impossible to express the real injury or the deepest, darkest obscurity of one's emotions in so many words.

OSTERMANN: I can express my emotions, but not my injuries, the injuries to my soul . . .

MÜNCH: But those are feelings as well . . .

OSTERMANN: . . . which cannot be put into words. How can I explain to you that I still can see myself treated as a subhuman species, like a vermin, not like a human being? These things one does not forget. I believe we have arrived at a point in our dialogue . . .

MÜNCH: . . . where nothing more can be said.

Wiping the Slate Clean?

INTERVIEW WITH DR. HANS WILHELM MÜNCH

Dr. Münch was interviewed by the producer, Bernhard Frankfurter, and his assistant, Karin Jahn in Munich in 1994. The following is a transcript of this interview:

FRANKFURTER: Let me ask you a question. How did you live afterwards with having experienced Auschwitz? For example, the desire to distance yourself from it and then the urge, even a compulsion perhaps, to deal with it?

MÜNCH: No, there was or is no compulsion or urge but merely a sober, totally rational consideration as I tell myself. This phenomenon—Auschwitz—has few equals in the history of mankind but only because its scale is so immense. There were many genocides in the course of history. But that something like that could occur in our enlightened, civilized times and that—as becomes more and more obvious—many enlightened people and nations, who prided themselves on their unblemished humanitarian record, did nothing to resist this genocide of European Jewry... these are experiences that I can teach to others, that are not available anywhere else, because there is hardly anyone who would have survived if he had been in my shoes. The few that still exist have remained invisible.

FRANKFURTER: After your acquittal, how did you come to grips with your experiences? Talking to your family? Or perhaps you had a circle of friends and acquaintances who put questions to you? Or did everyone sweep it all under the carpet?

MÜNCH: They certainly swept it under the rug. My friends talked to me about everything, only not about this topic.

FRANKFURTER: What motivated you to go public with the topic?

MÜNCH: Actually, it was Hermann Langbein who caused me to do it. I don't exactly recall the point in time, but he convinced me, instilled in me a sense of responsibility that I could no longer escape. After Langbein had written his book *Menschen in Auschwitz,* he decided that writing books was not the way to reach the people; there had to be a better way. In the first few years after the war, many people were convinced that something like that must never again be allowed to happen, and everything must be done to prevent it, such as through in-depth information. At that time many people did not believe what had happened. And many more did not want to believe it, because after all Germans with any patriotic fervor did not want to be identified with that past. There was only one thing left for them: to sweep it under the carpet, to close their eyes. But that was not the right way to handle that.

FRANKFURTER: And what conclusion have you reached? Writing does not seem to help . . .

MÜNCH: There is a real need nowadays. There are many people who listen to statements that Auschwitz did not really exist, that the gas chambers never existed, etc., etc. They believe that only too readily. It is very difficult to find a way to reach people. To simply confront them and say "I was there; I have seen it," that won't do it at all. You would have to find some motivation; I don't quite know what . . . This whole Yugoslav war situation, for example, that shows me anew that with cold reasoning nothing can be achieved. Therefore, if I analyze it correctly, I am probably driven by my emotions to continue publishing.

FRANKFURTER: What kind of emotions?

MÜNCH: That is hard to say. There is somehow a moral obligation, but that is only a word again. I simply cannot define it.

JAHN: One more question. You kept saying to Ms. Ostermann, "I find it so difficult to talk to you. You, as the victim, have it much easier." Do you really see it like that?

MÜNCH: But of course, that is the way it is.

JAHN: I fail to understand why you believe that a victim has less problems speaking about it?

MÜNCH: About Auschwitz?

JAHN: Yes, about Auschwitz, but also about another situation. Imagine a situation in your life in which you have been absolutely humiliated, robbed of all dignity and humanity. A situation in which you were powerless and could not defend yourself. Would it be easy for you to talk about such an experience? Or did you never have such an experience?

MÜNCH: No, I never did have such an experience, but I cannot imagine that it would be difficult to talk about the fact that one failed at one time or another.

JAHN: We are not talking about failure but about a person being completely debased.

MÜNCH: I understand. I know what it means to be told you are less than dirt. That situation I experienced in prison with the lower ranks who let us know, in no uncertain terms, that we were lower than dirt. That we deserve to be hanged and that we should be treated before the hanging, exactly as we treated the victims.

JAHN: And you find it easy to talk about that?

MÜNCH: Not very difficult.

FRANKFURTER: Tell me, what meaning does this conversation have for you, since you know that it will appear in a publication?

MÜNCH: It is no special pleasure. People ask me all the time: "Why don't you write something yourself?" Because I think it is impossible to tell it in such a way that people who have not experienced it themselves can even try to grasp it. To speak normally about this matter is already abnormal. I keep trying to speak about it as objectivly as possible. It gets better with the passing of time, but it also gets worse, because I keep telling myself: "It just can't be true that you have seen and experienced all this and did not break from it." At this point I have to explain something. If a person gets into an extreme situation, such as, for example, the people who lived through the nightly bombing in the large cities, he talks about it today as if he is talking with friends in a bar. At the time it happened it was a matter of existing and surviving. That is something so out of the ordinary, that it is hard to comprehend today. And with Auschwitz it was the same in a different way. When I came to Berlin after a big air raid—I went to Berlin frequently—I was staggered, really—what a horrible sight this was. But, after having seen it later several more times, it became almost normal. You only asked yourself how come some places burned worse than others? Do you understand? You start thinking about things like that very rationally. It is impossible to describe it or write about it.

Nevertheless, I feel obligated to report all I have seen as objectivly as possible. Any prisoner who writes a book has to first overcome a big handicap, the handicap of having survived at all. The only way he could have done that would have been if he had a special position. But in that case he cannot report from the point of view of the average prisoner. I had the opportunity to have seen not merely both sides, but also to have almost perished by being in between both sides. I consider it an obligation. I try to visualize it: in another fifty years, how are people going to think about this? The facts remain the same, the figures will be common knowledge, but you won't see the the human beings behind them. And then the public will read the books that have been written from the viewpoint of the prisoners in special positions; that is not very objective either. The readers of today will choose what appeals to them out of the narratives, and the rest will be small talk about old times. But what I really feel, I simply cannot tell; I cannot do that. Talking about numbers and dates, that does not transmit any reality either, not at all. Langbein seems to have the same problem. He really tried very hard. He tried to report objectively about Auschwitz. But he himself told me, "With a book you can only make them understand numbers. If you want to make them understand the human aspect, that can only be done through the arts." I do feel obligated. I was the only one acquitted. My wife hates the whole thing. My children, however, are very supportive.

FRANKFURTER: Was your wife ever in Auschwitz?

MÜNCH: She was. That was also a crazy thing. Before I came to Auschwitz I was assigned to do medical examinations for army inductees in Breslau. So Mrugowski said, "I would advise you to have your wife come to Breslau. In Breslau she can visit you but not in Auschwitz." I still did not know what Auschwitz really was. "That is a prohibited area," he had said; that was all. So I called my wife to come to Breslau. After a few days the order came: transfer to Auschwitz. So we looked in the train schedule for the best train from Breslau back to the Allgäu. Very simple, via Prague. So she went with me until Kattowitz and from there a train went via the Czech Protectorate, but that train did not run. So she went on with me. I said: "No problem, I know Weber." So we arrive in Auschwitz. The Unterscharführer from the Institute is there. "No problem," he says, "Weber won't be back until day after tomorrow, but we have plenty of room. No problem." So she came with me to the Institute.

On the way from the station to the Institute we saw the first column of prisoners on outside work. That was a strange sight indeed. It was a Sunday and the Institute was quiet; the prisoners were not there. The Institute was closed Sundays. Monday morning they marched in. The Kapo made his report. They all stood at attention and I said: "At ease." I was not used to military drill. I went up to each one individually and shook hands with them. The Unterscharführer, and even the prisoners looked at me as if I were crazy. Later on he explained to me that, under no circumstances, was I to have any direct contact with the prisoners. That's how it was. When my wife left, she was totally bewildered.

JAHN: Mrs. Ostermann had asked you if your wife had been an ardent Nazi, and you did not answer the question . . .

MÜNCH: My wife never was a party member, and she was never involved. That she approved of the reigning anti-Semitism that is certain. That had to do with the experiences she had with Jews in school, etc., though it is common knowledge that she had a few, good Jewish girl friends.

JAHN: But she was against you serving in Auschwitz. You yourself just said she was shocked when she left Auschwitz.

MÜNCH: Well yes, I had to really explain to her and promise on oath that I would never be personally involved in anything and that anything inhuman, demanded of me, I would reject, even if there were consequences to it.

JAHN: You were often home on leave, weren't you?

MÜNCH: Yes, I was often at home.

JAHN: And you talked with her then, of course.

MÜNCH: Always. It was always the topic.

JAHN: And now?

MÜNCH: Now she says: "I've had it up to here; I can't stand it anymore. I am tired."

JAHN: Does she feel she is being dragged into something that does not concern her at all?

MÜNCH: Of course. And from where she stands, she is totally right. My point of view is hard to defend, in her eyes.

JAHN: Would you call her, then or now, a supporter or an opponent of the Nazis?

MÜNCH: She never was a supporter, but she was also not an active opponent—just like she never was an active anti-Semite.

JAHN: Would you say she wanted to keep out of politics?

MÜNCH: Absolutely. Her father had been an officer, and her mother came from a merchant family who never wanted to have anything to do with politics.

JAHN: To change the subject, let us assume that you would be once again in the same situation. You would have the good fortune to be declared UK [indispensable] as country physician. Having had the experiences of your past, what would you do?

MÜNCH: I really cannot answer that.

JAHN: From what you told us so far, you just simply learned early to adapt to everything, to keep an eye on your future. After all, you did not study these many years for nothing. And then you had the great good fortune not to have to go to the front, and you sat securely with your family in the country . . . What I don't quite understand is why you wanted to leave there at all costs. Talking to Mrs. Ostermann, you said you felt embarrassed that the colleagues for whom you substituted were at the front.

MÜNCH: That was the obvious reason. Actually I had bought into the prevailing hysteria—how did they say it? Germany must win the war, or Germany is finished—that propaganda worked on me too, I guess. It doesn't do for a young man to be playing country doctor when the fatherland is endangered. These were the thoughts that kept nagging at me.

JAHN: And you were not afraid to think what would happen if Germany won this war?

MÜNCH: No, of course not, because I had no idea of the existence of the "Final Solution." I knew, of course, what Hitler had said in his book *Mein Kampf*, etc. But no one I knew took that seriously. I certainly did not.

JAHN: But at the time when you made the decision, so many people had already disappeared ... those who were able to emigrate, and those who simply were taken away.

MÜNCH: I never experienced that. I was not in any city, and in the country you did not see any of that.

JAHN: But even in the movies, the newsreels, you could see it. The excesses against Jews, the smearing of the Jewish store windows, etc.

MÜNCH: That people were against Jews?

JAHN: Yes.

MÜNCH: Well, I must admit here that I had a very bad opinion of Jews from personal experiences. When before the war a position was open for a young physician, it was always the Jews who would get the position.

JAHN: You know that from hearsay?

MÜNCH: No, from experience.

JAHN: But you got all the jobs you wanted immediately.

MÜNCH: That was, of course, when all the Jews had been kicked out, but before that time you would get nothing. I also have heard that from my mother's family, where there were many physicians. There are statistics for that, believe you me.

JAHN: Talking to Ms. Ostermann, you made a definite distinction between the Jews who had resided for a long time in Germany—you yourself had a good Jewish friend named Leo Oppenheim—and those who had emigrated from the East and brought with them, according to you, a different culture. The established German Jews, those were not the ones having come from the east, isn't that right?

MÜNCH: No, of course not.

JAHN: It would appear that there had to be a generic anti-Semitism in your family from way back.

MÜNCH: There is no doubt about that.

JAHN: And how do you look at those facts [preferential treatment of Jewish doctors] today?

MÜNCH: Well, as I said, I myself was never confronted with such a situation, but I knew of some actual cases where that had happened. Let us say, in the medical profession, the Jews represented a much larger percentage than was demographically justified.

JAHN: What I want to know is, what you think about the situation today, after you had told Ms. Ostermann that for you there is no such thing as *the* Jew or *the* German or *the* anyone.

MÜNCH: Yes, that is one of the experiences Auschwitz has taught me. But I fail to understand your question?

JAHN: I hear over and over again in conversations with general fascist overtones, "Well, of course we should not have murdered all the Jews, but we should have kept them from holding certain positions, etc." But no one among such groups could explain to me what they actually thought a Jew was: a member of a religion or a member of a race. There was always that double talk, those clichés. And what you are saying now has the same feeling.

MÜNCH: Of course I thought a lot about all this in the meantime, and I have come to the conclusion that there was no other way for the Jews but to stick together in the face of that worldwide anti-Semitism. That included, of course, not to let anyone else in when they had established themselves in some place. And it is obvious, that if a Jew became head of a clinic, and if he had to choose between two equally qualified applicants for a position, the one a Jew and the other an Aryan or a German, he would choose the Jew. And that the Jew was better qualified was a given, because as a Jew he had to work much harder to get into a university to start with. Even before the exam he had to prove himself better by his own achievement, simply because the deck had been stacked against him.

JAHN: Let me come back to my previous question. What would you do today if you were put into the same situation?

MÜNCH: I would act completely differently today... As I said, at that time I was under the strong influence of the Nazi propaganda machine.

JAHN: And when did you change your attitude? There was first of all the shock of the events at Auschwitz, but that may not mean that your mind-set changed immediately. That does not happen that quickly.

MÜNCH: I cannot really pinpoint that. But one thing I must stress: in my personal life racial considerations never played a part. I never had a personal aversion against Jews.

JAHN: One thing always amazes me: on the one hand there is the grand idea, the general concept, or if you like, the official version, the regulation. On the other hand, in the private sphere, we find the the exact opposite.

MÜNCH: Do you mean in Auschwitz?

JAHN: No, everywhere. During the Nazi period this fact becomes pretty clear. A perfect example is the fact that the highest rulers of the regime certainly did not conform to the Aryan ideal, neither physically nor in any other way. Or the position of women during that period. The official motto was: "Back to the kitchen [The three K's of Bismarck: *Kinder* (children) *Küche* (kitchen) *Kirche* (church)] and the reality was that all the women worked in the war industries. Or one is a ardent anti-Semite but has Jews for friends. How do you explain these contradictions?

MÜNCH: That is something I cannot explain. C'est la vie. If you accept your life, you cannot live by principles alone; you must try to stick to facts. That's just the way it is; among the intelligentsia, Jews have played a disproportionately larger role than they were actually entitled to. Why that is so, is another question.

JAHN: My question actually concerned something else. There is on one hand ideology, on the other reality, on one side regulations, on the other the practical application, and they just don't fit together. How would you handle any perfect ideologies or intellectual systems today?

MÜNCH: The more perfect they appear, the more skeptically I would approach them. I principally do not follow any religion or idea because

I am aware that human design contradicts any of that. If a state or an organization functions, then it is merely through good management, never through any pretended ideals or ideologies. Of that I am firmly convinced; that is my personal viewpoint.

JAHN: Well, now we are at the next point: management, that is, the duress to commit certain acts. You repeatedly stressed the problems you had to cope with, such as the mountains of corpses that had to be burned because of the real threat of an epidemic.

MÜNCH: Yes, of course. The extermination camps in the east, which had previously done the largest part of that work, had been closed. Now Auschwitz had to be adapted to do the big job. Our installations were only for domestic use, so to speak. Now our crematories had to take over for all the crematories lost in the east, with their entire capacity. The Warsaw Ghetto, etc., those were still being handled in the east. What came after that, of course . . . From the African Front they were worried that the Balkan would have to be given up, so they sent all the Greek transports to Auschwitz, and our capacities were absolutely overburdened.

FRANKFURTER: The transportation of deportees took precedent over the military transport. Was there ever any discussion of that, i.e., about the interests of the Army and/or the SS?

MÜNCH: The general assumption was that the SS always came first. It was said that the army was not as reliable as the SS. However, I never heard any talk about the deportations taking precedent over Army transports. That was no topic for discussion. The only topic was how to cope with the whole mess. There were these Head Kapos who came from Majdanek [extermination camp farther east] and who had mastered the technique. They were in demand. They were the people in charge. No one in Auschwitz knew how to build a pyre.

FRANKFURTER: Can you explain what a pyre is?

MÜNCH: Because the capacity of the ovens was overtaxed, and they were partially broken and insufficient anyway, we had to do something else to burn the corpses, because burning was the only possibility left. And so they used the experience from Majdanek. There they had already worked with these so called pyres. They would dig a big pit, and in it they would build a sort of frame on which the bodies were layered in heaps. We did not know how big the pit and the frame would have to be, what kind of fuel to use. Once it burns, that's fine, but there must be the right draft from the bottom, that means that the ditch will have to be constructed a certain way. That was the problem, because we did not know the technique. And as a doctor, I certainly would not know about that.

FRANKFURTER: Supposedly children and babies were burned alive on these pyres . . . Anybody ever talk about that?

MÜNCH: No. Certainly not. And if that would have been the case, I am sure no one of my rank would have approved of that. But at the time we speak of, it was more important to have the technique available than to worry whether someone was burned alive or dead.

JAHN: It is most incomprehensible that the technique, the "duress," could then and can be today so totally separated from the questions about the cause of these things. How do you see this in today's society? We also deal with "duress" situations?

MÜNCH: There is no difference between Auschwitz and now. I know this sounds strange, but I do not see any difference. I can't think of a fitting illustration right now . . .

JAHN: . . . Let us say the economy. No one would oppose the pursuit of a positive economic development in Europe . . .

MÜNCH: . . . and in Africa people are dying, that is obvious. A totally immoral attitude, and everyone contributes his share to improve the European situation.

JAHN: And only a few will say—with complete impunity—that these things should be changed; nothing will happen to them. It is looked upon as "duress," because if we do not strengthen Europe we will all perish. That is not actually true, but that is the way it is represented.

MÜNCH: I know, I know . . .

JAHN: What conclusions—after your experiences in Auschwitz—would you draw from that?

MÜNCH: I compromise, as long as it does not bother me too much. As they say: I howl with the wolves. In Auschwitz, that was another matter. There I was deeply moved and shocked by the human misery.

And I did the best I could to counteract it. But that you could not do at all, if you publicly opposed them.

JAHN: It would seem that basically nothing much has changed. Mrs. Ostermann repeatedly reproached you for having contributed to the smooth functioning of the Auschwitz machinery in spite of all your protestations. If there had been no external solution—through the war—that situation could have continued forever.

MÜNCH: One could do a lot with small deeds. That is what I tried to do, and that has been acknowledged. No one stepped up and said: that is all a lie; that is not true.

FRANKFURTER: Whatever may have been your personal behavior, by your function alone you were a member of the perpetrator's elite. On the other hand, there are the victims. What are your thoughts about the relationship between perpetrator and victim? And, in your view, is there such a thing as a slow merging, "a sort of fellowship" of these two positions?

MÜNCH: I am in personal contact with ex-political prisoners but only with those with whom I had been in contact in Auschwitz already . . . Others have never approached me. I did not go after them either, because they were not my concern. My concern is only with those who try to sweep that under the rug.

FRANKFURTER: For instance, in the Hygiene Institute, where there was a special prisoner commando—that was of course an exceptional situation for Auschwitz—was there anything resembling a coexistence between SS elite and the prisoners—was there a sort of working community or a survival community?

MÜNCH: If you are thinking of something like that, then I have given you the wrong impression of that situation. These were purely personal contacts. Aside from me, Delmotte also had several purely personal contacts with prisoners that eventually led to friendships. Even Weber had some contacts that were quite personal. But for many prisoners of my commando I was simply the person to talk to when they had a problem, for instance, when one of them wanted to help a fellow prisoner but in his position had no way of doing it. Or if he had found out that one of his relatives in camp was in great danger, he would ask: "Could you not help me to arrange something?" That was an everyday matter, nothing special in our coexistence there.

FRANKFURTER: Give me an example.

MÜNCH: Seen from today's vantage point they were all very little things, nothing big. For instance, there was one prisoner who had a very large hunger edema [severe accumulation of fluid in tissues due to starvation], and he was on the way to becoming a Muselmann and needed some milk. The question was not merely to get the milk but to get the milk into the camp. That was when I could use my influence. I was not the only SS member to do that, because the fraternization effect worked everywhere, even among the professional criminals. When I was in prison in Cracow after the war, a lot of my fellow prisoners [SS] there bragged about all they had done and how many prisoners they had helped . . . Probably most of them did the favors for some prisoners in Kanada, from whom they wanted something.

FRANKFURTER: Did you have any contact with prisoner physicians?

MÜNCH: Of course, continuously. I had to check on the hygienic situations in the camps, in the camp hospitals. Of course, those were rather perfunctory, very superficial checks, because there was no sense in doing that. They would keep undercover anything they did not want us to know.

FRANKFURTER: How did that actually take place?

MÜNCH: We would go into the hospital compound, and the head prisoner physician would report and salute. We would say: "How is it going? Do you have any problems?" Then they would start talking, but they would exaggerate of course: "We are totally out of ether." Then I would say, "That is not our department. We are only responsible for the hygienic conditions." "But we could use the ether mixed with other medications as a disinfectant, and disguised like that, couldn't we get the ether?" That was the usual form of conversation with prisoner physicians. If the prisoner physician was sure that we did not try to get him in trouble, but that we wanted to support him in his efforts to treat as many prisoner patients as possible as well as possible, then we sometimes could do such things in agreement with Dr. Wirths. Because if Wirths did not know of any way out, he would turn to us to "organize," illegally, some things he needed. The word "organize" was the keyword for everything in camp. Everything was in short supply, and if one wanted something, you had to get it illegally, and that was "organizing;" that was the way of life there.

FRANKFURTER: But there was a certain method to that madness, because through these stratagems things were running fairly well.

MÜNCH: You had to be aware that the actual rations, distributed, were quite a bit smaller than the ones received to be distributed. That happened of course because the prisoners who sat at the source, [in the warehouses, in the blocks, where the rations were received] organized first of all their slices off the top, so they could survive better. That was the way of things. Of course the others had to make do with less.

FRANKFURTER: The SS allowed that, didn't they?

MÜNCH: Of course they did, because they depended on the Kapos to have everything running smoothly. If the Kapo did not keep things running, then the next in line, the SS man who supervised the Kapo, found his life to be all the harder. But that was only one of the sources. Another source was that, among the SS troops, alcohol was always in short supply. So, if one had a way to obtain alcohol, for instance, he could go to the slaughterhouse and tell his fellow SS man in charge of the slaughterhouse: "I have two bottles of vodka; what do you offer." Then the other one would say: "Ten kilos of sausage," or something like that. Perhaps there would be a bit of bargaining, but in the end the slaughterhouse would once more be short so-and-so much sausage.

FRANKFURTER: Let us continue with the hospital compound. The hospital compounds were a special institution within this Auschwitz system.

MÜNCH: An institution under Dr. Wirths where the camp commander had absolutely no say. That opened up quite a few opportunities to play out one against the other, just like in real life.

FRANKFURTER: For example?

MÜNCH: Let us assume Wirths finds something to complain about in the hospital compound. He goes to the camp commandant and says, "Such and such has got to be changed. We need an additional barrack for the hospital." The other one says: "Can't be done. I have no more barracks [pre-fabs]." Then Wirths says, "I have an obligation to the Hygiene Institute to see that the epidemic is being curtailed. I must have the barrack." The two of them then bargained that out between themselves. And if one or the other wanted a personal favor, that was also thrown into the pot. That is how that went, just like in everyday life. Only under extraordinary circumstances.

FRANKFURTER: Tell me about Dr. Wirths.

MÜNCH: Wirths was the typical functionary. He tried as best as he could to observe all the rules. That never quite worked, and so he had learned to make arrangements with people to obtain, for instance, certain medications from Kanada for his prisoner hospital. It was his hobby to furnish his prisoner hospital with the best material available, to get surgeons, to get them the equipment that they needed, so that they could do some interesting things.

FRANKFURTER: Experiments?

MÜNCH: No, no experiments. He wanted to be a gynecologist.

FRANKFURTER: How was the system of selections in the hospital compound?

MÜNCH: That was very complicated, and every case was different. If, for instance, the camp physician was lazy and the Kapo was very active, then the physician would leave everything to the Kapo. He would only say, "How many Muselmen do we have?" The Kapo would answer, for instance, "Fifteen." "Can we possibly cure them?" "No," said the Kapo. "They must disappear as fast as possible, because we need the beds for more arrivals." That was one way.

FRANKFURTER: In that case, the Kapo decided who was gassed.

MÜNCH: In that case, yes. At other times it was just the opposite. Let us say the camp physician was especially ambitious. He had a special interest—such as how to develop a better treatment for prisoners with diarrhea. He would make sure that as many beds as possible were available for the diarrhea cases. In that case some prisoners with pneumonia would have to "bite the dust." These things cannot be generalized, but in the last analysis the camp, physician was the master over life and death.

FRANKFURTER: Well, one thing is quite clear. The hospital compound was not really a place for people to get well.

MÜNCH: But it was. To put it another way, it did not merely exist to kill people, but to maintain as much of a viable labor force as possible. Of course, it was understood that other interests came into the picture, such as that it had to be as cheaply maintained as possible.

JAHN: To return to a question of Ms. Ostermann. Why did they not gas the psychologically and physically disabled Muselmen and use the new arrivals from the ramp or after the quarantine as work force?

MÜNCH: That always depended on the orders from above. If there was an order that said at least 30 percent of a given transport had to be gassed because we had no housing for them, then that was an irrefutable argument. Orders from above took precedent above all else.

JAHN: Was it not possible, perhaps, that the ones on the top did not have the right information? That there was no communication from the bottom to the top?

MÜNCH: Everyone passed the buck. Only people like Mengele, if he thought that something should be done, then he defied everyone. He did not give a damn. For instance, in the question of the gypsies, he changed his viewpoint several times. He said they all have to be gassed because they were not worthy to be alive. But before that he had said the exact opposite, that they must be maintained, because they are so artistically gifted.

FRANKFURTER: And Indo-European.

MÜNCH: Quite right.

JAHN: So, no one wanted to take the blame. But the people you were in touch with, did they not talk among themselves about the methods of selecting? That that—in the spirit of the goals of the SS—was totally crazy?

FRANKFURTER: There seems to be a simple explanation. The final aim of the whole enterprise was extermination. And at the time of the large deportations—such as the Hungarian ones in the summer of '44—they already knew that the war was not winnable in the normal way, and so they murdered the healthy ones immediately because the sick ones would die anyway.

MÜNCH: That's quite possible.

FRANKFURTER: It was known that there were certain techniques to make people in Auschwitz toe the line. Was that being taught? Were there certain courses being taught for that, or was the behavior simply acquired by being introduced to the practices?

MÜNCH: There was training in both these ways. First of all, there was the ideological training. These ideology professors would appear every so often to plug the party line. There would be a lecture and then a social gathering, a jovial party. That was an absolute farce. The subliminal suggestion was continuously pushed, that we, the SS in Auschwitz or the death head unit in general, were doing the hardest work for the war effort. "And be assured, you will be compensated when we have won the war," we were told.

FRANKFURTER: In the official day rooms, the canteen, officers' mess, were there the usual slogans on the wall, such as, "My honor is loyalty," etc.?

MÜNCH: Of course. Up until the third glass of beer these slogans were loudly proclaimed while standing at attention. After the fourth glass it became a drunken brawl.

FRANKFURTER: What kind of slogans were there?

MÜNCH: All about standing firm, mostly. I don't remember them in detail. We hardly ever attended. At times it could not be avoided. It was the usual routine. It was not any different at the SS in Auschwitz than at the local chapter number so-and-so in Hintertupfing [invented name for hicktown or village]. Meetings like that were already degenerating at that time. Already the last big party rallies before the war were almost as degenerated as the Olympics are today. They have nothing to do with sport anymore, that is nothing but a big show, a business. All organizations are like that. Most things that grow out of an idea become corrupted and perverted and end up serving some personal interest.

FRANKFURTER: Were you already in Auschwitz during the Warsaw Ghetto uprising?

MÜNCH: I never knew anything about that. That happened farther east; we in Auschwitz had nothing to do with that.

FRANKFURTER: Did you know at all that the uprising had taken place? Did you have any information?

MÜNCH: No, only what was in the newspapers, and that was little enough.

FRANKFURTER: Was there such a thing as a special jargon among the SS?

MÜNCH: If there was such a thing, we probably all used it. But we were not aware that it was a special jargon. I could not really recall anything like that.

FRANKFURTER: Did you have any nicknames for the leaders?

MÜNCH: None whatsoever.

FRANKFURTER: For instance, what kind of image did Himmler have?

MÜNCH: For the ordinary SS man, Himmler was a God.

FRANKFURTER: Were there jokes about him?

MÜNCH: No, not at all. There were no jokes about Himmler. He was such an average person. He would not have allowed any jokes about him.

FRANKFURTER: But after all, he, the representative of a master race, was himself relatively small and puny.

MÜNCH: The puniest imaginable, a real grade-school teacher type. [In Germany and Austria that was the lowest and most disdained position a teacher could have].

FRANKFURTER: And yet no one made fun of him in the SS?

MÜNCH: No, no. For example, even Mengele indicated that Himmler was an impossible person, but . . . here I go mentioning the Catholics again . . . that would be like attacking the Pope, and that is not done.

FRANKFURTER: What did you and Mengele talk about?

MÜNCH: Just general talk. For instance: Can the Jewish question be solved by physically setting them on fire? Says Mengele, "That actually should not be done, but we have to do it, because other solutions are worse. We cannot send them to Madagascar and isolate them there. But something has to happen. And since we have no other way, we have to continue what we are doing. Because if we do nothing and let it go on as before, the German people are going to be destroyed and the rest of the world as well." That is the way Mengele phrased it. He was, to put it simply, a convert. He had been brought up Catholic, and suddenly he had decided this organized religion is all a bunch of shit. And then he fell for all of this primitive Nazi ideology. And then, unfortunately, he also lapped up the so-called genetic science,—a pseudoscience, like psychology—like a thirsty sponge. Suddenly he is given the opportunity to demonstrate his genetic theories on identical twins, a chance he would never have again. Because with laboratory animals he cannot experiment as successfully as with human beings. And so he slid into a path, were he perhaps realized something was not quite right after all. That is why he debated so much about it, because he was not sure of his direction. And now we find out that he led an absolutely primitive life in Argentina and that all his ideals had evaporated, and all he was concerned about was to stay alive. He, who had been so enthusiastic about his cause.

JAHN: You mention that genetics is a pseudoscience. How do you mean that?

MÜNCH: I was thinking of the transmission of acquired characteristics. What I mean is, if I educate people through several generations a certain way, then this way is transmitted through tradition, not genetics. National socialistic theories frequently mixed these concepts up. In genetics the question has always been: can acquired characteristics be inherited? I consider this a totally unfounded, unscientific claim.

JAHN: You said that Mengele lost his ideals. How is that?

MÜNCH: There was a Nazi propaganda machine active in Chile and Argentina among these people [tr. note: those of German or Aryan descent]. He distanced himself from them and never followed up on the strong convictions he held in that regard in Auschwitz. I would have expected him to be very active there, after all the heated discussions we had in Auschwitz.

FRANKFURTER: Do you see that as positive or negative?

MÜNCH: I do not understand it, that's all. That he fled overseas simply to stay alive, that he wanted nothing to do with his past. In Auschwitz he acted as—one can almost say—apostle for the Nazi genetic theory, one he was willing to die for. That was a disappointment for me.

JAHN: You ranged your colleagues into three categories: the order takers; the opportunists; and the convinced perpetrators, the true believers. Listening to you it sounded as if you respected the convinced perpetrators the most.

MÜNCH: They were the only ones that you could have any kind of discussion with.

JAHN: I am speaking here of respect.

MÜNCH: I have to admit I could not, and generally one really cannot, deny them a certain amount of respect, of recognition, if you will. Among convinced perpetrators, I understand those who were absolutely not opportunists. Mengele was one of the convinced ones. Well, I guess his conviction was not quite as firm, otherwise he would not have stopped with his work.

JAHN: He might have come to his senses . . .

MÜNCH: He was much too deeply involved. He could not ever have said, "I was mistaken." But he really was led astray. Just like Delmotte. I am corresponding right now with a woman who was very interested in Delmotte. She knows him from his childhood and knows that he was educated differently, but that he missed his father. When the father began to be interested in the son and pulled him towards the SS, she, as a Jewess, had to note how her playmate suddenly drifted toward the SS, in spite of his different predisposition and education. Delmotte then married a woman whom they sent after him to Auschwitz to help him with his problems. She fitted into that surrounding like a square peg into a round hole. She was super-elegant, in the most decadent sense, and she was a real fan of things American, just like Weber. Those two were happiest when they could talk together about America. Poor Delmotte just sat there. She was almost emaciated, very pale, very blasé, and loved to dress in black and white. She hardly ever said a word, only posed all the time. Once Weber came with a black and white great Dane—a degenerate beast, totally useless, as a watchdog—she saw this dog and annexed it immediately to use him as a foil for her looks. So she ran around with that dog on a short leash. That was the kind of woman poor Delmotte was married to. I really would like to know whether she was not part of the reason for his suicide. Because she left him.

FRANKFURTER: She ran away from Auschwitz?

MÜNCH: No. She was there only a few weeks. With the people from the SS casino, she did not talk at all. They were for her lower than dirt. But every other day she went to the camp, to the so-called hairdresser parlor, where specially selected prisoners cut the hair of the officers' wives. That too was a part of Auschwitz. One could talk forever about Auschwitz. Just the fact that we all were involved in an absolutely immoral institution. There had to be a point there, where one had to draw some lines. Where you said "that's all, I am not going along anymore."

FRANKFURTER: But that would mean that the going-along with everything also was part of the amoral institution.

MÜNCH: That is true. Once you're in it, you cannot get out. Either you put a bullet through your head, or you say, "You are all murderers," and then they put the bullet through your head. But if you play along, you have to set clear-cut limits. Whether I pretended to myself that I stayed within my limits or whether it was really so is debatable. But I really thought that I did help many people purely on the physical level, even some of them psychologically, to hold on, because they saw that not all of us were evil. Having to reproach oneself to have gotten into the situation by one's own efforts is of course a matter that everyone must work out with his own conscience.

JAHN: Did it ever occur to you that there might have been other SS men who at one time or another had contemplated resistance? I am thinking specifically of Delmotte.

MÜNCH: No, it did not. As for Delmotte, he seemed almost my personal enemy, because he had the much better opportunity to avoid selections, due to protection from higher up. But we both reacted alike—no selections. He had had the special intensive SS training; I did not have any of that. And even with this training he caved in after a short time, that was my luck. If it would have been any other way, I could not have avoided it. I would have had to find another way to get through.

FRANKFURTER: Meaning that you would make selections after all.

MÜNCH: No. That clearly was the limit.

FRANKFURTER: At that point you would have rather died?

MÜNCH: Absolutely. I could not have gone on living doing that.

JAHN: I would like to pick up on another question. You did talk with Caesar after the war, didn't you?

MÜNCH: Correct. Caesar would have been someone to talk to. But it never occurred to me to do that. I always took him for a fervent SS man, though I knew that he acted very decently in his camp. He had at least one to two thousand people under him. But it seemed inconceivable to me, that someone with that much fruit salad [meaning gold braiding on the collar] would not be a convinced national socialist. He had a hay drying installation in our area, but I would have never thought to speak with him privately.

JAHN: And after the war?

MÜNCH: We did talk after the war. He told me, "From the beginning, I belonged to Himmler's inner circle. We really built up our ideals together. And then I get involved in this mess and can't get out."

FRANKFURTER: He was not convicted?

MÜNCH: No.

JAHN: Another question. You rank your colleagues in three categories. Did you make such value judgments also for the prisoners? You talked about the Kapos, the gypsies. Can you range them somehow, like you ranged your colleagues?

MÜNCH: That is rather difficult. To put yourself into the place of the prisoner is extremely difficult. Don't forget, they were all such poor wretches, so dependent on all our whims, that you could hardly categorize them.

JAHN: But you repeatedly described how one or the other managed to get into a better position. There must have been different attitudes.

MÜNCH: That was always pure self-preservation. Everyone tried to do that. Some just had better luck than others. The circumstances were so unbelievably extreme that nothing else mattered but survival.

JAHN: Yes, I see, but why then did the story with the gypsies shock you that much?

MÜNCH: Those were not individual gypsies, who shocked me. The gypsies in general, their lifestyle, that's what shocked me.

JAHN: Then there was a difference there for you.

MÜNCH: Do you mean racially?

JAHN: I want you to tell me what it was.

MÜNCH: As far as I am concerned, the gypsies were without exception inhumane people. Among each other, to their children, their women. And the Klan elders were the worst.

JAHN: How do you know all that? From Mengele? Because you yourself only dealt with them with the Noma cases.

MÜNCH: No, no, I went several times through their camp. It was a completely different way of life from what we know. Maybe in the depth of Arabia there are such situations between the male rulers and the subjects. The gypsy problem in Auschwitz really touched me deeply.

JAHN: How do you see it today?

MÜNCH: If I encounter gypsies I give them a wide berth, as wide as possible . . . I don't want any contact with them.

JAHN: Did you ever try to find out how gypsies lived under normal circumstances?

MÜNCH: But they did live in normal circumstances.

JAHN: In Auschwitz?

MÜNCH: In Auschwitz. They lived in normal family situations. The families were not separated. They would have had sufficient food, guaranteed by quite a few people who championed the gypsies month after month. But they certainly failed to justify the kind of trust people had in them.

JAHN: If they were trusted that much, they did not have to be locked up.

MÜNCH: I phrased that wrong. It was not because of lack of trust that they were imprisoned but for their own protection. Not a one of them would have had to die.

JAHN: But why then were they imprisoned?

MÜNCH: Because they were dangerous; they did not cooperate. You could not rely on them. But the authorities realized that this was a valuable national treasure that had to be protected and that could only be done if they were interned first. The assumption was, of course, that they should be taken care of as well as possible.

JAHN: So then, in your opinion, the gypsies were gassed because they behaved badly?

MÜNCH: Of course. They rejected what was offered them. Even Himmler could not protect them anymore because the camp management was of the opinion that the gypsy camp was destroying everything in the entire camp.

JAHN: Did that also include the idea that Aryans behave better than non-Aryans?

MÜNCH: Could be, could well be. I don't remember anymore. But they were unbearable, unbearable.

JAHN: Another question. Among the prisoners, were doctors and chemists with knowledge about diseases that had long been eradicated in Germany. The SS used their knowledge if they found such specialists? How did they find them?

MÜNCH: First the doctors were sorted out for their medical knowledge as prisoner physicians. It usually did not take long until there developed between the prisoner physician and the respective camp physician in charge a certain collegiality, provided the prisoner knew his limitations. As a rule, a prisoner physician could always speak out stating his opinion and his experience.

JAHN: What I am aiming at is the fact that the whole system of fighting epidemics would not have functioned if it had not been for the prisoner physicians. That is what I was told.

MÜNCH: There really were just a few epidemics. Mostly from Eastern Europe. Take, for example, Noma. No SS physician knew anything about that. Or in Buchenwald. There they needed an expert for the spotted fever research. Mrugowski was informed; he then passed the request on to Weber. Weber then discussed it with Wirths, and Wirths made inquiries among the prisoner physicians. If they found one, which did not happen that often, that prisoner could really have a career ahead of him. Weber, for instance, got his institute staff together by asking, or having people ask at the ramp [incoming transports], whether among the transport there were any serologists or bacteriologists. When they had found enough of them, they did not ask anymore. Later on, in the Institute for Hygiene, we would ask among the prisoners: "Do you know of anyone who would be qualified to work here?" Of course there were plenty who claimed to be qualified, and they were not qualified at all. It was a heck of a job to finally find a qualified one. What we usually did was to get a prisoner physician and tell him to examine the applicants to find out who pretends to be an expert, and who really is one.

JAHN: But you yourself never did something like that?

MÜNCH: The fact that most of them spoke German very badly was the biggest handicap.

JAHN: That must have been an important question—especially in your commando.

MÜNCH: Even the lowliest prisoner tried his best to speak German.

FRANKFURTER: How was the food in the Hygiene Institute?

MÜNCH: There was so much that we produced ourselves that we took the food assigned to us by the officers' mess and handed it on to the prisoners. Bernhard, our prisoner cook, did not tolerate anyone in his kitchen. In our area we had enough space to grow salad and such; of course not we, ourselves, but the prisoner did the cultivating. Livestock, such as guinea pigs and rabbits, we needed to breed anyway, to produce "Wassermann" [a syphilis test] and all these things. We just bred more than we needed and butchered the surplus. Right from the beginning, Weber instituted that on his own. He delegated one of his subordinates to be responsible for our supplies. That was officially designated, supplemental nutrition. Our commando consisted of approximately 100 prisoners. The camp food for 100 prisoners was brought in every day in large vats. And we always donated additional food from our stores to the prisoners' rations. There was never anything left of the camp food. Even with our contribution to their rations, the prisoners really could not have done without the camp food, but we, the SS, could well do without the army food. The slaughterhouse really was dependent on us. All we had to do was just once not approve of a batch of cows that they got in there and they would be in a terrible fix, because they could not fill their work quota. That's the way it worked: one hand washes the other.

Not that we threatened each other, it was all on a friendly basis. There was a record of everything down to the last ounce, every bit of material that we had to examine to certify that it was hygienically pure. There were, for instance, several barrels of rotten orange marmalade. A chemist, one of the prisoners in the commando, had the bright idea to distill that marmalade and make alcohol out of it. The alcohol could be sold, and for it we would trade for sausage. That's the way it was done. That is just sort of a slice-of-life description of a corrupt society.

FRANKFURTER: I don't know whether you would call that only corruption. But more likely, like moonlighting in today's society, that is one of the survival techniques.

MÜNCH: True, but a very amoral survival technique. And in the extreme situations of Auschwitz, these practices also went to the extreme. For instance, the story with the tailors. That every one of the SS had an unofficial-official private tailor.

FRANKFURTER: Were those Germans or were they Poles?

MÜNCH: They were Polish workers, Polish tailors.

FRANKFURTER: In this connection could you also tell us about the story with the human flesh?

MÜNCH: We obviously always needed meat to make the culture medium. The Unterscharführer who was in charge of getting the meat from the slaughter house—it was substandard meat, that would be used for boiling—always had problems getting enough. Why? Because he probably also cheated somewhere. In such a fix it can be expected that you tell yourself, God knows there are so many corpses lying around, human corpses, why not cut a piece out of an ass and put it into the broth. Meat is meat. Pork is worse than human flesh because you have to render the fat first. There is no need to do that with human flesh. That seems to have been done long before my time; whether Weber knew about it or not, I don't know. And one day, when Weber was gone again, an Unterscharführer came to me and said, "We have no more meat, but we used to do that many times before. I need your permission so I can get it through Wirths." The man was dead anyway. Whether he now gave his flesh for bouillon or not, what difference did it make under the circumstances, that was the accepted way of thinking at the time. But I told myself, if that continues, pretty soon they will use nothing but prisoners' flesh and sell the animal meat to get more booze. That was my deliberation. And therefore I called Wirths and said, "This cannot continue."

JAHN: You have always said that everyone had dirty hands. Did you as well?

MÜNCH: By the criterion of the national socialistic ideology . . .

JAHN: But you did not adhere to that, right?

MÜNCH: No, of course not.

JAHN: You did say that you did not take the whole thing very seriously from the start. That you thought that the racial theory was an idiotic propaganda tool.

MÜNCH: What do you want to imply by that?

JAHN: What I want to imply is that if you reject an idea, a system, then it would not be immoral to act against it.

MÜNCH: You could not say outright, "that is a rotten mess you are doing there." You had to go along with it to start with. Luckily the Institute of Hygiene commando was there somewhat taboo, untouchable. They were all specialists, they could not off hand do away with them. Human beings, the prisoners, were not very important. Only if one of them was indispensable, then he would attain some kind of esteem as a human being in the camp. The normal prisoner was simply material, to be used or rejected. And when he became a Muselmann then he slid even lower. But if that Muselmann knew a Kapo from earlier times, who was willing to go to bat for him, then even the Muselmann could be helped by that connection. Everything in that camp was connections. Every branch, every small camp area had different rules and connections. It was a different world in general, but totally corrupt.

FRANKFURTER: Was not the corruption an integral planned part of the system?

MÜNCH: Probably not planned, but unavoidable. The survival instinct reigns supreme. I experienced it myself later in the Polish prison. That was not exactly a vacation.

FRANKFURTER: How long were you imprisoned?

MÜNCH: From '45 to '48, three years. But I experienced it already in the prisoner of war camp, where we were crammed in under very primitive conditions. The camp direction tried to bring order in there, and they needed experts to do that. When someone was an expert in something, he had a chance. I had seen how that worked in Auschwitz. I had no problems to find positions in these large camps where they needed a special expert. I knew the routine that the others did not. I knew how things worked in a prison camp. I did really well in these circumstances, simply because I knew what had to be done and that it was not even a matter of knowing but simply of pretending to know what to do. For instance, I had some experience with sculpting. One night some drunken American comes into the camp. He is looking for someone to help him. He had a broken plaster bust of Hitler, and he needed someone to put it together again. I was listening to him, and I said, "That is no big deal. All I need is a bit of clay, and I can make a Hitler bust like that easily." Two days later, I had all but forgotten about it; I am called to the commandant. And there they were with the clay. So I made the Hitler bust, that came out all right. So for two to three weeks I did nothing but sculpt Hitler busts—with the right kind of material, and they even would be fired—and the Americans sold them. Something else came out of that. They selected all the painters among the prisoners to show what they could do. They gave them brushes and paint and they had to paint, that standard picture of the roaring stag in the forest wholesale, and those they also sent to America to be sold. I only tell you that to show you what advantage it was to know the ropes. In Poland then, that was different. That was a real prison. The best one could do there was to become a barber.

FRANKFURTER: And did you become a barber?

MÜNCH: No. I had a much more interesting experience. One day I am called to the investigating judge. He said to me, "I have not dealt with your case yet, I really do not need to do it either. You have been cleared to a large extent. But I do have a problem. In cell number so-and-so, in solitary confinement, sits the last governor of Cracow. He is an old man, and we should actually release him, but he is mentally disturbed. He had been posted to Cracow toward the end of the war, where his predecessors had been butchers, and he was supposed to smooth things over. He really did try to create a measure of normalcy there. He had the best reputation possible. But he has gone completely crazy because he feels guilty. Reads the bible constantly and does not understand it. You are a physician, aren't you? I would really like to

put you together with him. Maybe you can straighten him out a bit."
So he put me in the man's cell, but it was rather hopeless. Two days
later they came to get me from there. "What do you think?" they
asked. "I don't know what to do; perhaps, if you give him something
to do, some kind of work." "What kind of work?," they asked. "I
know of something," I said, "In the Hygiene Institute in Auschwitz we
have crates full of examination notes. If they would still be there,
perhaps he could make some kind of scientific work out of that material." Two days later, the crates were here. We set to work sorting the
notes. On these notes were written: 1. the prisoner's number, from
which we ascertained his arrival in camp. 2. the diagnosis, from which
we could see if he was perhaps already a Muselmann and probably
did not live very long. And with enough of these figures one could
eventually develop some kind of statistics. The old man attacked that
task with great fervor. He sorted, and I sorted too, and we made
statistics, of sort, out of it. And the result, an incredible parabolic
curve, showing health and life expectancy. When the prisoner arrives
his life expectancy is optimal. The statistics show exactly how that
changes. I handed the results to the investigating judge, and he handed
it to the hygienics experts at the university of Cracow. Among them
were quite a few former prisoners whom I happened to know. I had
hardly been released when I received a big letter from the former
prisoner organization in Poland stating, "We finished your research
about the life expectancy in Auschwitz, and we would like to publish
it." The sad part of the story is the old gentleman had to stay in prison
longer than I because there simply was no mechanism to release him.
After all, you cannot let the Nazi governor of Cracow go free without
finding anything against him. He had to stay two more years in prison,
and then was sent home. He was a very decent gentleman whom the
Nazis used to sway public opinion in their favor, before the Russians
came. And he really tried hard to seriously change the mood in Cracow,
and what does he get? Gets captured by the Americans and is treated
like dirt.

FRANKFURTER: How long were you in solitary?

MÜNCH: Not long at all.

FRANKFURTER: Were you interned together with any SS colleagues?

MÜNCH: Nothing but. I must admit, I would have liked to be imprisoned with Höss, he sure would have been more interesting.

FRANKFURTER: You never did have any personal contact with Höss, did you?

MÜNCH: Not in Auschwitz. He was much too high-up. Besides, Weber made sure that we would have no contact whatsoever with the camp management. But he liked being in Auschwitz because there he could do the work he liked.

FRANKFURTER: He preferred a large measure of autonomy, no?

MÜNCH: That's right. He really came there in spite of the commandant. But the spotted fever had come across the fence with such rapidity that the troops were endangered as well. Before that, they had always thought all they had to do to stop the epidemic was to lock the barrack doors and set fire to the inmates within. That did not work at all. It only led to the prisoners hiding any spotted fever case. When they found one, they would do away with him themselves.

FRANKFURTER: Let us go back to your imprisonment. You said you were together with other SS men. How was life in that prison?

MÜNCH: First I was in an SS barracks in Kornwestheim near Stuttgart. All the time some commissions of former prisoners would come through there—I knew none of them. We had to line up; they inspected us, and, from time to time, one of the SS would be taken out. Mostly little people, guards. They would be transported out. I was told later by the investigating judge that a lot of the former prisoners recognized me, but told the judge: "We don't want him, we have nothing against him."

FRANKFURTER: What kind of people were there with you?

MÜNCH: Only normal, simple SS men. None of them ever said he was in a camp.

FRANKFURTER: You never were together with any responsible officers?

MÜNCH: Only later in the Polish prison. There the prime defendants were partly in solitary. All the others, of course, never did anything, according to them. They only "did their duty." Everyone would tell about his merits, which that one, or the other one, "that pig" did not have. You understand what I mean? You could see right away what kind of types they were. Then there were the simple foot soldiers, many Ukrainians among them. They stuck together and played chess. Of course, they did not have a board and chessmen. They simply called out numbers to each other. The crowding was indescribeable. Everybody had a blanket; the nutrition was barely sufficient, but nobody starved. There even was an infirmary in the prison, with a Polish doctor in charge. This Polish doctor was 1. a Jew, 2. no doctor at all. He had been an orderly, not in Auschwitz but in one of the satellite camps. He had learned a considerable amount of medicinal knowledge, spoke German quite well, and put on a big show there. After not too long a time, he suggested I should assist him. Thus I did my best to help maintain the health of the prisoners, so they could be tried. The Poles were, of course, very interested in that. I did quite well there doing that. That pseudo physician who had been in the camp for years and years was a real slick customer; he knew all the tricks, and even I could learn a few from him.

FRANKFURTER: Of medical knowledge?

MÜNCH: No, but how best to survive a camp. He also was responsible for the families of the prison guards. They were housed in a special area, and I had to go with him when he made his calls there. Since I was a German physician, I counted for something with them. He interpreted and also gave me advice on what I could profit from the whole affair. We did that for quite a while. The payments for the calls were in vodka, and the guard who went along to guard me got the liquor. Of course, the commandant was kept in the dark about that. Then the whole thing came out. It seems the doctor had treated one of the higher-ups in the guard personnel for a cut he had got cutting bread. He bandaged the hand correctly and put the thumb in a splint. Unfortunately the tendon had been cut.

FRANKFURTER: He overlooked that?

MÜNCH: Right. It was a simple cut, and the tendon lay high up. In any case, the man could not use the finger anymore, and he would have needed it for shooting. The so-called doctor recognized that immediately and kept him placated with compresses and soaking, to gain time. Then he told me what had happened. For him the job would be finished; imagine, a Jew having crippled a Polish soldier. That just wouldn't do. Did I perhaps know how he could get a job in Germany? And with that he disappeared. When I was acquitted in Cracow, I was not immediately released but was put into a special section of the prison. I could not get in touch with anyone. There I associated with a Kapo, from a camp near Danzig. He was a criminal, a very pleasant fellow; his name was Paul. He was a longshoreman by profession. Those long-shoremen must have been a special category of men. He was very humane, a darling fellow, but totally depraved. He had passed through a lot of prisons and then came into the camp as a green [criminal] Kapo. He had been afraid that the other prisoners would kill him at the end of the war, so he dug himself in under a heap of corpses and stayed there. I found him very interesting. This man had grown up in that surrounding and had never seen anything else. He and I were sent to Germany together, to the vicinity of Stuttgart. There we were relatively free. We just had to stay there until our papers would arrive.

JAHN: In your trial judgment, it states that you had been forced into the SS.

MÜNCH: That is not quite true. There the Poles have different ideas. For them there are only two categories: the active, voluntary Nazi and the other ones, who simply—like in the church—belonged. That is how they saw me.

JAHN: They did not interrogate you at all about that?

MÜNCH: I can't remember.

JAHN: And the story with Strassburger?

MÜNCH: They did not care about that at all. For them it was only impor-tant that I was in the quasi mandatory category of membership, a fellow traveler, so to speak. And in the eyes of the Poles that was no crime.

FRANKFURTER: Have you been in Auschwitz since the war?

MÜNCH: I would have liked to go there once to see the Museum, but everyone, especially the Polish prisoners with whom I was in touch, told me, "Do not go there, if you know what's good for you. In spite of your acquittal, they prefer not to see you, because you do not fit into the frame that the museum likes to show." There were quite a few prisoners who did not approve of the Museum.

FRANKFURTER: Let us come back to your acquittal . . .

MÜNCH: At last the papers arrived. I was released and took Paul with me in May '48. I was almost afraid to come home by myself, and Paul, he just started crying, to see a family like mine. He soon got news of his own family and left for Hamburg.

FRANKFURTER: Did you stay in touch with him?

MÜNCH: No, I am sure he landed in prison sooner or later.

FRANKFURTER: And how did you fare?

MÜNCH: My wife worried about my future. She said, "You just need to listen to the radio. There is one man in the Jewish Community who makes such vicious talks against the SS; you'll never have a chance. On Friday at such and such time you can hear him." I am listening: a certain Philipp Auerbach is speaking. He really opens his mouth wide. But that is Philipp, one of the camp characters par excellence. I took him into the commando from a delousing station towards the end of '44. He pretended to be a chemist. How much of a real chemist he was I never knew. He had been the owner of a shoe polish factory in Belgium, a very educated man. He had been taken over by the Hygiene Institute. He had not been particularly well-liked by the old prisoners. Since Weber was not in charge anymore at the time, he had asked me to help him not to be transferred to the general camp. When I heard him on the radio, I knew I had no need to be afraid. He was the representative of the politically and racially persecuted refugees. He later became a drug addict and died miserably. He really tried to help so many people and made so many promises, that he could not possibly keep them all . . .

So I go to his office, a long line of petitioners ahead of me at his office door. Well, I think, I'll just go home again. But then I open the closest door to get some information. Inside a man sits behind a large desk and looks at me. My God, that is Hecht, another one from my commando. He was a very young boy at the time. He practically hugged me and took me immediately in to see Philipp Auerbach, and Philipp was also happy to see me. He immediately sits down and dictates a letter to his secretary that designates me as a political refugee qualified to receive financial support. I still have that letter.

We Are Still Here

INTERVIEW WITH DAGMAR OSTERMANN

Ms. Ostermann was interviewed by the producer, Bernhard Frank-
furter, and his assistant, Karin Jahn, in Vienna in 1994. The follow-
ing is a transcript of that interview.

FRANKFURTER: Let us start with your teen years. Even before 1938 you
were frequently in Germany...

OSTERMANN: I visited my family in Dresden quite often. I experienced
Nazi Germany before Hitler came to power. After the war, when my
uncle said: "We knew nothing," I reminded him of that period, saying,
"I can well remember when I was in Dresden in 1928 and 1929. At that
time, the Nazis still marched in rather small groups, called the
Brownshirts, and they sang, Jew blood must spray from our knives...!
You can't tell me, since you yourself were in the NSKK at that time,
that that did not mean anything."

FRANKFURTER: How was it for you after Hitler came to power?

OSTERMANN: I had a foreign passport, so for me it was not threatening,
because, first of all, I did not know a single Jew in Dresden. All my
friends knew that I had a Jewish father, but that was no problem. I
even knew guys who were in the NS Labor Service, and one of them,
I remember, was in the Hitler Youth. And some cousins, boys and

girls, were in the Hitler Youth and in the BDM. But I was considered their equal; my whole family was really just average, no better and no worse than thousands of others, perhaps a bit more susceptible than others. But they all loved me.

FRANKFURTER: But when you walked through the city, with Swastika flags everywhere, there was a certain amount of propaganda . . .

OSTERMANN: That was not too obvious in Dresden. That was one of the reasons why my uncle wanted to take me there in 1938, because the atrocities and mistreatment of Jews that were happening in Austria he had not noticed in Dresden. The Jewish community in Dresden was relatively small; the Jews were not in any upper-level positions, they were just merchants. I never saw a store being smeared with boycott slogans in Dresden.

FRANKFURTER: Were you in Vienna in '38?

OSTERMANN: To start with I was. In '38 I was in a business school, had been there since fall '37. Before that I was an apprentice with the firm of Goldscheider, in their office. But since I did not like it there at all, because all I had to do was make breakfast and go shopping for the office, never doing any office work, I stopped working there in '36. My mother always agreed with what I chose to do. But this time she said: "Listen Dagmar, if you don't want to work there, then you will go to business school in fall." But then came a letter from my grandmother who had had an accident, and so I spent half a year helping her and came back in January of '37. On March 12, 1938, when I came to my business school, the business college Allina, the brownshirts were already standing guard at the door, and the school was locked since the Allina brothers, the owners of the school, were Jews. Everyone was hoping to get out and abroad as fast as possible. I would have had the papers for an au pair job in Brighton, but my mother said, "No, you are not leaving. If you go I shall never see you again. Who knows what can happen?" That is how I missed my escape.

FRANKFURTER: What were your first impressions of the so-called Anschluss [annexation of Austria by Nazi Germany].

OSTERMANN: I was in the Café "Börse" with a young Jewish friend of mine, a physician, and we heard Schuschnigg's abdication speech and a few minutes later the "Heil Hitler" of the announcer. Of course, we left immediately; he went home to his father, a butcher in Hütteldorf, and I to my mother in the Kolingasse. Within half an hour all policemen already wore the armbands with the swastikas. They must have all had them in their pockets already—and they demanded identification of everyone in the street. My mother said, "Let's see what is happening." We went down around 9:30 p.m. Mother and I passed by the Creditanstalt [Vienna's largest bank, founded by the Rothschild family], and there for the first time, I realized the horror to come. There was a wiry, slight man, a civilian with a swastika armband, and he was in the process of beating another man who had no swastika armband, had dark hair and wore glasses, while he called him, repeatedly, "Dirty Jew." The dark, dark-haired man, though slight, must have been quite strong, and he hit back and said: "I am no Jew, but even if I were one, you have no right to hit me." That was typical for that period. If you had dark hair and dark eyes, or perhaps a larger than normal nose, then you were fair game. All this happened not more than an hour and a half after the abdication of Schuschnigg. And the next morning on the way to school, I already saw Jews kneeling on the sidewalks with toothbrushes and scrub brushes trying to wash away the Krukenkreuze from the sidewalk. And the good citizens of Vienna stood around and howled with delight. At the pastry shop "Lehmann," even before it opened for business, the next day there already hung a sign "No admission for Jews and dogs." That was on the morning of March 12, around 8:45 A.M. On March 14 or 15, my uncle Alfried marched into Austria with one of the first German Army units. He wore his army uniform and came with his own motorcycle with sidecar. He had requested permission from his commandant to stay with his sister.

FRANKFURTER: What rank did he have at the time?

OSTERMANN: Corporal.

FRANKFURTER: Not an officer . . .

OSTERMANN: Never was. His last rank was sergeant. He was no academician either; he was a tailor. Academicians were only on my father's side. Only one uncle on my mother's side, the husband of one of her sisters, was a famous scientist, whom I liberated after the war in Pirna. Because my uncle stayed with us, our apartment was, of course, off limits for any raids. All of the people who had greeted us in a very, very restrained manner after the Anschluss suddenly were overly polite again. Like all the military, my uncle, of course, bought everything he could lay his hands on. They robbed poor Austria blind. They pretended to want to help us with their Bavarian supply train, in spite of the fact that we had things they could only have dreamed of in Germany for many years: gold, flour, sugar. I remember how they sent enormous packages back into the Reich. The business people, of course, were delighted; business was booming. They did not realize that they were at the end of the boom, and whatever came after this, they would have to buy and sell on ration cards. My uncle really enjoyed himself, but for the first time in his Nazi career, he saw the excesses in the streets. He saw how they loaded Jews and opponents of the regime on trucks. He saw them marching out of the Rossauer Barracks [the Gestapo prison in Central Vienna] where they deported them in cars and trucks to the Concentration Camps. He also noted things going on in our apartment house. That was when he became worried about me, and told my mother he was taking me to Dresden. That was in April '38. He got me a military rubberized suit like the truck drivers wore, while he wore his steel helmet. Then he put me into the sidecar. That is how I emigrated to Germany instead of emigrating abroad. I stayed with my aunt Lydia in the Erzgebirge. My uncle often came by to take me along on his border patrols. At the parties, I was usually the center of attention, the blond, blue-eyed Viennese. Nobody knew of my Jewish father. Things went fine like that for two or three months. Then my grandmother broke her foot again, and I went to Dresden to help her.

I had a nice circle of friends already: one friend, a Czech citizen, who knew that I was half-Jewish. At that time I did not know that the Aryan laws would cover me too. My friend and I were ready to get married and were already announcing the bans. Ten days before the wedding, Czechoslovakia was declared a protectorate of Germany, and the racial laws were in force there too, so we could not marry anymore. But this boy really stood by me. He was summoned once or twice to the Gestapo, where they told him to break off with me immediately. But he took no notice of their request. My friends also stood by me. They had known me since I was a baby, and they were marvelous. On the day when I was ordered to wear the star, they were furious: "How mean can they get to make Dagmar wear the star." Some of them were very embarrassed. They simply could not believe it. They had read and heard a lot, but they had not taken it seriously. We lived in a working class neighborhood. I remember that well, because before Hitler all the flags in the windows displayed the hammer and sickle flags of the Socialist party and a few black-red-gold ones. Only from the window of our apartment flew a swastika flag. After 1933 they all had became more or less Nazis. That was how it went then. But my grandmother never turned Nazi. She always said, if you attack the people of the Lord, then fire and vengeance would rain down on you. And fire really did rain down on Dresden. She never could understand why some of her children went in that political direction. She was a pious Christian and, besides that, she hailed from Eastern Prussia [Famous for stubborn individuals].

FRANKFURTER: When were you summoned to the Gestapo?

OSTERMANN: August 18, 1942

FRANKFURTER: Was that when your uncle had been there, and they had told him to advise you that it would be best to hang yourself?

OSTERMANN: Yes, that was uncle Erich. Then came the day of the interrogation, and, fortunately, uncle Alfried was on leave at home. He told my mother: "I am going with Dagmar to the Gestapo. Don't worry. I'll bring your child back." At the time, he was a sergeant. He went with me to the Gestapo office; there was a long corridor, a few steps up, and a reception counter. This also was called "Hotel Metropol," just like the famous Gestapo headquarters in Vienna. They always used very good hotels for the Gestapo. That hotel in Dresden does not exist anymore. I handed in my card, and opposite the reception counter there was a group of chairs where my uncle sat down. I was going to sit next to him, and the guard yelled immediately: "You wait in the hall." There I stood with my star. The door into the hall opened; the officials there pushed me and spit at me as they passed by. They did not know that the sergeant sitting there was with me. I signaled to my uncle not to get into an argument with these people. After about two hours, they finally called me to the second floor; I don't remember the room number. The room was bright and had a desk in it. I just remember the name of one of the men; it was May. The other one's name I have forgotten. In the right corner was a closed door; on the left side an open one. There sat an elderly official called Chief Inspector Pohlhas. No one talked to me. Mr. May ate an apple and offered his opinion about me to his colleague: "Wouldn't that be a sweet piece for a bit of Rassenschande." Suddenly the closed door opened. That was the first time that I saw someone in the black SS uniform. He was an Untersturmführer, and he said, "You know why you're here, don't you?" And I said: "No, I don't." And he said, "How do you keep in touch with your mother?" And I answered, "By letters." And he said, "Not true, you telephoned her on the 22d. at such and such time, from the railroad station." I could not deny that. Then he began asking me about the Coffe House Lunz, the place where I used to secretly meet my old friends from time to time. I wanted to answer him, but he interrupted me. "You don't have to tell me anything; we know all about you." And he disappeared. Suddenly the phone rings next door, and the chief inspector yells loudly, "Tell him to come up immediately." And then he yells at me: Your uncle has gone crazy. He wants to talk to the Obersturmführer." But at that time the army uniform was one of the sacred cows in Germany. My uncle comes into the room and the chief inspector Pohlhas says to him, "Well, Comrade, you're really in luck that you are wearing a uniform. Otherwise you would not find me so friendly." And my uncle, who was absolutely furious that he had to wait for so long, said to him, "Now I am going to tell you something Comrade. I was already a party member when you still shit in your pants." They were all very embarrassed at that and sent me out of the room again. And suddenly the three officials come out of the room with my uncle—and now you shall see again the stupidity, that blind belief in the regime—and my uncle says to me: "Dagmar, pro forma they must put you in jail for a week, so they would not be accused of playing favors for my family." And I said,

"You really believe that?" I knew from the factory where I worked that anyone who had received a summons never came back. But he said, "When an authority like the Gestapo gives me their word of honor that you will be out in a week, I must believe them. After all, in Germany, thank God, a man's word is his bond." That was after he had already seen that his niece had to wear a Jewish star, had to have Jewish ration cards, worked in a Jewish department of a factory, and got arrested. And nevertheless he was capable of making remarks like that. So they took me to the Gestapo prison in the Schiessgasse, in Dresden. That prison still exists. There I was put into a cell with a pickpocket and a prostitute. Our numbers increased in the cell. Even a few women with stars came in. During the first week, they came to get me every other day and sat me down in a sort of office. There sat a youngish Gestapo official who was very friendly and unctuous. He said, "We would really like to help you because of your family, but you would have to help us a little as well. You are living with Jews now; you should be able to hear or see a few things . . ." They wanted me to become a Gestapo informer. But that was out of the question. I had a good excuse however, "All the Jewish people there know about my family. So they never talk in front of me about anything incriminating because they are afraid I would talk to my family. Whether they handed over all their property to the Gestapo or whether they are in touch with any Aryans I just don't know." So the first week passed, then the second week. My uncle was back at the front. My aunt was allowed to bring me fresh clothing. Towards the end of September, I was called out of the cell during the night and taken into an office. They gave me a paper saying "protective custody order." In contrast to some other such orders, I was going to see later, on my order no offense was listed. I signed the paper. It would have made no difference in my fate, if I hadn't signed.

Next morning when I was taken downstairs, there were nine or ten other prisoners standing there already, all without Jewish stars.

My dark blue coat with the Jewish star attached, which my family had brought to the prison, lay on the side. I put it on. Then we were taken with a prison car to the train. In the train, there were prisoner compartments on both sides: the right side for the women, the left side for the men. Doors and windows were barred. The guard contingent were German policemen, not SS. We were brought to Berlin, to the prison on Alexanderplatz. That prison was so overcrowded that we slept in the hallways for two days. It was the collection point for all prisoners from German cities. From there, they distributed their victims to the various camps. Then we were put into another of those barred trains. This time only women.

FRANKFURTER: What kind of women?

OSTERMANN: People always think that only dangerous political prisoners or racially persecuted people were sent to the camps. But that was not so. For example, with us there was a girl in a peasant dress, shaved bald. Her father had had an argument with a neighbor; that neighbor denounced him to the political official of the county because supposedly the girl had slept with a Polish indentured laborer. Without even examining the girl, whether she had ever slept with a man—she was only 16 years old—she was shaved and paraded through the village with a tag around her neck saying, "I am a German who has forgotten her honor. I slept with a Pole." And without a trial, she was sent to Berlin-Alexanderplatz and now with me to Ravensbrück. By comparison with my later quarters, Ravensbrück was clean and orderly. I wondered why they did not put me into any of the working commandos. On the third or fourth day after the evening roll call, an SS Rapportführerin came and said: "All of you with stars stay outside of the block after the roll call." The blocks had Jews and non-Jews in them. We were told that we had to be on the roll call square the next morning because we were transported out. We were not told where to. We were not allowed to take anything but our tin food bowls and spoons and the clothes we wore. They took us to the train in Fürstenfeld, the train station for Ravensbrück. The same prisoner trains waited for us, no cattle trains, but the guards were SS this time. As there were windows, we could see that we were moving in an easterly direction. There was much excitement and tension, and that brought us all to a complete collapse, and we fell asleep. Suddenly the train stopped with a jerk:" Dallidalli, [German equivalent of "Move it"] out,

out." All I saw were barbed wire, arc lamps, and guard towers. I did not know where we were. We did not arrive in Auschwitz proper but in Birkenau on the ramp. We only walked a few minutes through a gate, and there we had to stand along a fence next to the gate. The SS left; it was sort of twilight. On the camp street we saw indefinable figures. We could not tell if they were men or women. And suddenly a figure approached us. She looked like a walking skeleton; she seemed to consist of eyes only. She asked us where we came from. We said, "From Ravensbrück," and then we asked, "Where are we here?" And she said, "You are in Auschwitz." That was the first time I heard the name Auschwitz.

FRANKFURTER: When was that?

OSTERMANN: That was on October 6, 1942.

FRANKFURTER: You already talked about your early camp experiences. How about describing some of the other conditions in the camp, such as sanitation, for instance.

OSTERMANN: Sanitary conditions were atrocious. The latrines in the women's camp at that time were rectangular cesspools enclosed by concrete strips about 30–35 cm wide. You really had to sit far back on the concrete to hit the cesspool. And these emaciated female muselmen would frequently fall into the cesspools and did not know how to get out. And since we could visit the so-called shower rooms—where not a drop of water would come out of the showers—as well as the latrines only with the blockälteste, if she said, "Off with you, hop to it," you had to leave, whether you were finished or not. And, of course, there was no saving the ones who had fallen into the cesspool. We had neither towels nor paper, no rags to clean ourselves, no soap, nothing. There was a certain method to this madness. We were supposed to look dirty, filthy, disgusting. Our nicknames from the SS and the administrative prisoners were "Pigs," "filthbuckets," etc. These were approximately my first impressions. I was sent to a Jewish block. There were no bunkbeds there, only bunk palettes, three tiered, about 1-by-$1^1/_2$ meters wide and deep, so that you had to lay in them with your knees drawn up. There was one straw sack in these bunks and one blanket. And according to how many people were put into the block, there would be six to ten people in one of these bunks. Of course, you were like sardines: body to body. The next day I already had lice and, later on, spotted fever. That was when I first heard about the gas chambers. "No one can survive that" was my first reaction. My neighbor said to me, "What do you want? You want to survive? Either you starve, or you are beaten to death, or you get one of our lovely epidemics, or you go to the gas." I could not believe that. I argued with them. "But that is not possible; you cannot gas people." If I could not believe it being there, I can well see how people living far from there could not believe it either.

FRANKFURTER: You then worked in the Political Section, in the registry. What function did you have there?

OSTERMANN: My only function was to write death certificates. According to the file card, the particulars were added with the typewriter—name, date of birth, place of birth, cause of death. The form would be signed by one of the SS doctors. I drew the lines between the entries on the death certificates. They were made so no one could add anything to the document. From October '42 to April '44 I did nothing but draw lines between the names, dates, etc.

FRANKFURTER: Did you have anything to do with the Hungarian transports?

OSTERMANN: No. By that time I was already in Birkenau, in the penal commando.

FRANKFURTER: How was it when you were put into the registry office?

OSTERMANN: In the beginning that was rather difficult. The other prisoners were suspicious. I could have been an informer. Only weeks later, when they saw that I was a good comrade and of good character, did they accept me.

FRANKFURTER: And how did you survive the spotted fever?

OSTERMANN: I really do not know how. I did not go to the dispensary for one single day. I did not get one single dose of medication. The only thing my comrades did for me, they charred my bread ration on the little potbellied iron stove we had in the office "till it was like charcoal, the type you would buy in the pharmacy to combat the diarrhea, which, of course, was also a part of the disease. And we had two male prisoners there, Aryan Poles, and they would organize some black tea that they would give me. That is how I survived the spotted fever, as well as malaria and typhoid fever. Never one day in the hospital block. And that with good reason; the SS doctors made frequent selections there.

FRANKFURTER: There were also hierarchical levels among the prisoners. Did anyone try to play up to the higher functionaries?

OSTERMANN: No. On the contrary, but there were some very decent Kapos. You simply cannot generalize. Just as there were some very decent Blockälteste. And some very rotten, simple prisoners as well. But it was a sort of unwritten law not to be too closely connected with someone in power.

FRANKFURTER: Who was made Kapo? Were there any psychological prerequisites?

OSTERMANN: That is hard to say. Especially looking at it from the position I had. Thank God, I never had to deal with such a situation.

FRANKFURTER: With your position in the Political Section, did you feel somewhat more protected than others, in spite of the continuous threats?

OSTERMANN: We never thought of it that way. We always knew that in the end we would be finished as well. After all, we were secret-bearers and for that reason probably destined for the gas. If they would not have needed us some fine day, we would all have been in the gas. We always hoped, but the sword of Damocles hung over us day in, day out.

FRANKFURTER: Did you become cynical in that situation? Did thoughts such as what is the value of an individual and such cross your mind?

OSTERMANN: We had no time for philosophizing. Our philosophizing consisted of surviving from one day to the next.

FRANKFURTER: Did you ever notice any SS man who might have shown that his nerves were shot or who might have had some guilt feelings?

OSTERMANN: No. Never. If one of them were a bit more humane than the others, I really can't say whether he had been humane to begin with.

FRANKFURTER: Was there ever any rumor about any problems between the SS people?

OSTERMANN: We never heard anything of that. I only heard about some of the things much later. We only knew when one of them was gone. But why he had left or was removed, we never knew. Of course, there was always a rumor mill going. But the gossip was mostly about people you did not like. That one is guilty of that, and that one did that, etc., Kapos mostly, for example.

FRANKFURTER: Did you ever find a current newspaper lying around, such as the *Völkische Beobachter* [official Party organ]?

OSTERMANN: No, never. Though sometimes we would get information or hear rumors from fellow prisoners who worked in outside commandos or in the factories. Sometimes the civilian workers there would tell some news. But that would only concern the events at the front, never Auschwitz itself. The things that would have made the SS look bad or the revolts and such things I only learned later through postwar literature. We only learned of things that happened in Auschwitz proper, such as when a prisoner escaped, and we had to stand for a long roll call . . .

FRANKFURTER: Who did the executions in the Bunker?

OSTERMANN: The SS

FRANKFURTER: And the Kapos?

OSTERMANN: The Kapo in that block who was responsible for feeding the prisoners was a prisoner. But the punishments, such as the shootings at the black wall, were handed down and executed by the SS. They would have never put a gun into a prisoner's hands.

FRANKFURTER: How about eroticism and sexuality in the camp?

OSTERMANN: That could only happen with great difficulty. Because if an SS man showed sympathy for a Jewish prisoner, as it happened once to me . . .

FRANKFURTER: In Auschwitz?

OSTERMANN: Yes. There was a certain Unterscharführer named Willi Hoyer. He was from the Sudet area of Czechoslovakia. He did interviews in the Political Section and got prisoners from the registry office to record the interviews. He used to call for me frequently. First he would give me something to eat, and then he would try to get tender. And I always said, "Unterscharführer, you will be sent to the front and I to the gas. This is Rassenschande." "No," he used to say, "no one will know it." At that time Perry Broad was still in the Political Section. He loved to play the accordion, mostly American Jazz. That, of course, was strictly forbidden, as a civilian you could be sent to the camp for being caught doing that. Anyway, he happened to be practicing in that barrack, because he thought no one was there. And that was my salvation. I believe love affairs between SS men and Jewish prisoners were rather rare. That there were affairs between prisoners, I know for sure. As a matter of fact, when I was in the penal commando, there was an Aryan prisoner who was highly pregnant.

FRANKFURTER: A political prisoner?

OSTERMANN: No, an "asocial" one. She had refused the Nazi work assignment for her. We became friends, and when the child was born she named it after me.

FRANKFURTER: And the child lived?

OSTERMANN: The child lived until Mengele got his hands on it. He probably must have made some of his experiments with that blue-eyed Aryan child. When they brought it back to her, its eyes were totally red. It died within nine months, one day after the Russians liberated the camp.

FRANKFURTER: So the child was protected at its birth?

OSTERMANN: Of course. The father was an Aryan political prisoner, and the mother was also a German. She did not have to go to work; she was given a recuperation period. And the child was then taken to the children's block, where they even had some cribs for the children.

FRANKFURTER: To come back to the sexuality? Was homosexuality common, as it usually is in prison situations?

OSTERMANN: As I mentioned before, there were lesbian women prisoners among the "asocials" in the penal commando. Maybe there were some lesbian affairs among the Jewish women as well. To tell you the truth, I myself had absolutely no desire for any sexual encounters. The continuous pressure, the hunger, the bromide, which they supposedly mixed into our soup, suppressing the menstrual cycle, contributed to that asexuality.

FRANKFURTER: I would like to change the topic for the moment. Was there something like humor, like jokes in the camp?

OSTERMANN: We really did not feel much like joking. But, of course, we sometimes laughed about some things that happened, things that girls talked about in the evening sitting on the top bunks in the Stabsgebäude dormitory.

FRANKFURTER: Such as. . . .?

OSTERMANN: Well, sometimes we had to stay longer in the registry office because there were so many death certificates to process. Then, of course, we did not come in time for the supper ration distribution in the Stabsgebäude. Four girls were then designated, mostly by us, to go into the men's camp [Auschwitz I] to get a kettle of soup. And we always chose those girls who were the most appealing to the men and who could best organize. And it always worked. They sometimes would put whole pieces of meat into the soup, they also sometimes gave us sausage. The girls would put the sausage up their sleeves or hang them around their necks. No one would notice a stiff walk, because we were supposed to walk very stiff and straight. Or they would give us margarine. We wore these striped flannel underpants. We would sew elastic in the bottom of these so we could stuff those underpants with bread and margarine and the elastic would hold the stuff. The SS man who accompanied the group was distracted by the fact that he himself was busy organizing in the men's camp kitchen. Once during the Greek transports, they even gave us Halva. We stuck that in the pants too, and of course, it was sticky. Those were the things we laughed about.

JAHN: What kind of kitchens were there?

OSTERMANN: There was an SS kitchen and a prisoner kitchen, institution-size kitchens both.

FRANKFURTER: Where does the expression "Kanada" come from?

OSTERMANN: I suppose it was thought that Kanada was the land of plenty, that's why.

FRANKFURTER: And Mexico?

OSTERMANN: Because it was so far away. [Actually, the camp B III, in Birkenau, was so named for the colorful summer dresses the Hungarian prisoners had been given and their habit of wrapping any available blankets around them during the morning roll call to keep warm, which made them look like Mexicans with serapes].

JAHN: There really seems to be some sort of gallows humor in these designations.

OSTERMANN: As prisoners we did not see it that way. The actual camp jargon originated with the SS, such as "If you don't toe the line, you'll be soap," or "You'll be roasted." That jargon is still with us, and I find it outrageous. People still say here, "He fell through the roasting grate," meaning someone is dead.

FRANKFURTER: And the prisoners did not have any jargon? Perhaps about the food?

OSTERMANN: Well, yes. The disgusting brew that they called tea, we called acorn water. Otherwise, I can't think of anything.

FRANKFURTER: You were in the penal colony, weren't you. For how long?

OSTERMANN: In April '44 I was sent to the penal block in Birkenau. That was where our work consisted of "moving mountains," as I described it. There I stayed for a few months because you were assigned to the penal block for certain periods of time. Then you were sent to a normal block and put to work in an outside commando. Our guard was an awful man. He did not do anything to us, but he yelled continuously. He was drunk most of the time and laid down in the bushes. Working in that outside commando I met a Viennese SS man who had come to the SS at a rather late date. He heard me talk during the work as we were leveling a former carp pond. That was hard work. And he asked me, "Where do you come from?" And I said, "From Vienna." "Come sit down with me" he said, "and watch that the others work. But they should only work if another SS comes by." He then would bring me sandwiches every day. After the war, when I went for the first time to the Maxim cinema in Vienna, I saw him standing at the ticket window and I said to another former prisoner who was with me, "Say, isn't that Erwin?" He was afraid and ran away. I wouldn't have done anything to him because he was kind to me. I don't know what else he had done in camp. He had black curly hair. He looked like ten Jews, according to directives of Streicher, the publisher of the "Stürmer."

FRANKFURTER: How long did you stay in Auschwitz?

OSTERMANN: On November 1, 1944, we were put into a transport, this time in a cattle car. That was the first time for me. They told us we were going to Ravensbrück. I was delighted to hear that, because I thought it would still be like it had been when I left there in '42. I calmed down my fellow travelers. We arrived in Ravensbrück literally filthy and shitty. It was freezing cold. The trip from Auschwitz to Ravensbrück was twice as long as the trip to Auschwitz from Ravensbrück, because of the frequent bomb attacks. We went from the train on foot to the camp. We were stiff with every piece of clothes frozen on us. We were put into a gigantic tent, because the camp was overcrowded with prisoners. In the Middle of December '44 a commission arrived. They selected 500 of us for Malchow, a small satellite camp of Ravensbrück. That was a small camp, very clean; they used to have foreign laborers in there.

FRANKFURTER: You were liberated on May 2, 1945. What were your feelings when you saw the SS being taken prisoners by the Americans?

OSTERMANN: That was the strangest thing. I could not have cared less. All I was interested in was how to get home.

FRANKFURTER: There were many former prisoners who broke under the experience of Auschwitz . . .

OSTERMANN: Yes, there were many who broke under that past, though not immediately. I had a Dutch friend, for example, who was always psychologically rather fragile; we always had to protect her. She always had her head in the clouds and wrote beautiful poetry. I heard she published a book after the war, but she was finally put into an insane asylum. I had another comrade; she was a very strong person and also wound up in an asylum. I believe she expended all her strength in the camp. She was the protector of many of us and therefore had had no time to become depressed about her own fate. A few years after the war, she broke under the accumulated and unresolved stress of the past. But there are still a few who will not come forward; there is still a certain amount of fear that they have not come to grips with.

FRANKFURTER: Was it not hardest for the artistic temperament to cope with the past? Paul Celan and Jean Amery and other artists committed suicide, didn't they?

OSTERMANN: That is easily explained. I believe they all broke under the post-war experiences. They saw that the rest of mankind had not learned from their story, their experiences. They all were very euphoric immediately after the war when they started writing their poetry, their perceptions of the experiences. But then they saw that all their writings, even the depositions of the SS, were not enough to make mankind learn from history. All these artists committed suicide in the seventies.

FRANKFURTER: How do you cope with it?

OSTERMANN: I am simply too obstinate to be afraid. I firmly believe that we cannot teach the older generation anything, but I am enough of an optimist to believe that if I teach the young people, something will stick with them. When I go to speak in the schools, I continuously get letters and statements that make me believe if I even reach 10 or 15 percent those few might be able to work for some change. If we today do nothing at all, we must not be surprised if something happens again. Not that it does not take a lot out of me. The older I get, the more photographically intense my memory becomes. I see the images before me: the marching columns, the muselmen. I shall never forget the eyes of these muselmen. That is all they were, walking skeletons, with only the eyes still visible in the skull, and many times these eyes were like dead eyes. They only came alive when they saw a drop of water or a piece of bread somewhere they could get to without being caught. I virtually see my father standing in the column and walking to the gas chambers. And when my son says today, "Mama, why do you keep doing this? You have to look after your own mental and physical health." I answer him, "I was spared and survived for a purpose, and as a consequence of that survival I have an obligation." Of course, this is also a double-edged sword. You open wounds of the soul, but by talking about it you psychologically let go of a piece of the past, also.

JAHN: I observe time and again, that the perpetrators cope with it easily because they feel that they have won, while the victims cannot find a way to live with the damage to their human dignity. How did you manage that?

OSTERMANN: In the beginning, after arriving in the camp, I felt terribly ashamed. But I realized from the beginning that all they wanted was to demoralize me. And then I got stubborn, thinking to myself, "You shall not succeed." And after it was all over, I had nothing but feelings of triumph: "You did not succeed."

JAHN: How did that sit with the SS when a prisoner like you showed some spine?

OSTERMANN: Well, Unterscharführer Kristan once called me into his room because of something he objected to; I don't remember what it was about. He was about to hit me with a folder in his hand, and I looked him directly into the eyes; and he put down the folder. I fully believe if I had cringed, he would have hit me. But I was in a special commando, the secretaries of the SS. In Birkenau all my stubbornness or my spine would not have helped me one bit. As an ordinary prisoner on outside work and dependent for nourishment only on the camp food, being exposed to rains and snow, ordered around by the SS and the Kapos, I would have lost my spine pretty soon. One of the main conditions in Birkenau's outside commandos was "don't make waves."

FRANKFURTER: During your present, everyday life, do you ever have any flashbacks to Auschwitz?

OSTERMANN: Not now any more, but right after the liberation, I used to break out into a cold sweat when I saw a uniform, whether that was a policeman or a postman. And I cannot cope too well with large crowds. Even today I don't like to go to a department store. I would get agoraphobia. Today it is not that strong anymore, but I still don't like crowds.

FRANKFURTER: While you were married, did you talk about your past?

OSTERMANN: Certainly, all the time. My husband was also Jewish and had fought with the partisans in Yugoslavia. We talked a lot about our past. Also in my circle of friends, whenever my friends from the camp and I would meet, we always had the best intentions to talk about fashions or cooking or family. But 30 minutes later, the topic was the camp again. But when I want to talk to my son about it, he says,

"Don't talk to me about this; I know all about it. Talk to the others who don't know it." I once asked him why he will not go to any film dealing with this topic, and he said, "Look, all these things connect with you in my mind, I think that all this was done to you. And if I look at any of these partisan films, I think of my father having experienced that. That provokes such feelings of aggression in me that I would be capable of beating to a pulp the next person who makes an anti-Semitic remark to me." Actually he has already been fined twice for something like that.

FRANKFURTER: How did you and your husband look at the normal Austrian world?

OSTERMANN: We never knew the totally normal Austrian world. We chose our friends very carefully. To my husband's regret, I always was up-front with new friends. When we met someone, they should know right from the start who we are. I never believe that Austrian anti-Semitism was put aside with the lost war. In the beginning it was not done to be an anti-Semite. But anti-Semitism always existed, even if dormant, and today it is "in" again. Jews were always aware of it, because they have had hundreds of years of experience with it.

FRANKFURTER: Today, when you look at your TV and see in the news that nations are again setting up camps, like in Yugoslavia for instance, what are your thoughts on that?

OSTERMANN: It distresses me terribly. It is again the innocents that suffer. Again we see what has happened so often in history: different religious groups have lived peacefully together for decades, intermarried, have done business together, and then some political hotshots are looking for power and, to satisfy their ambitions, embroil a whole nation in a war. But, nevertheless, neither there nor anywhere else are there any phenomena like the gas chambers.

FRANKFURTER: What, in your view, are the important things in your daily life?

OSTERMANN: Moral courage. For instance, I am sitting in the trolley #58, three people get on at a station, two women and a man. One of the women looks out the window, and says, "Pretty soon you will not be able to go shopping on the Mariahilfer Strasse [Main shopping street in Vienna, 6th District] and the Taborstrasse [Main street in Vienna 2d District] is already jammed with Yugoslavs." That remark so outraged me that I could not keep myself from saying, "Well, here we go again. Before the war it was the Jews that bothered you, now it is the foreigners." Where upon the woman looks at me and says, "I did not talk to you, did I?" And I said, "I could not help overhearing what you said, and perhaps there are some foreigners here from the U.S. or Switzerland, etc., and they go back home, and they tell their people, 'No point visiting Austria, they hate foreigners.'" And suddenly the whole car sided with me, and the three people got out at the next stop.

FRANKFURTER: Have you been in Auschwitz since the war?

OSTERMANN: Oh yes. Once I was with a group of former inmates, also from Ravensbrück, and once with interested young people.

FRANKFURTER: You are strongly involved in lecturing in schools. How long have you been doing that?

OSTERMANN: For approximately six years.

FRANKFURTER: How does that affect you, always telling the same story?

OSTERMANN: It is quite an emotional stress . . . When I, for instance, imagine my father going to the gas . . . on some days I can stay calm talking about that, but on other days the tears well up in my eyes. If I ever would have the feeling that I would become too emotional, or if I would feel that I am not reaching the students, then I would quit. But as long as that isn't the case . . .

Thoughts on the Totality of National Socialism and the Extermination Policies

"What happened once, must never never happen again" is the repetitious motto of every public speaker at the recurring commemorations, the official and government directed "overcoming of the past." Just as the victims in the past would be neatly listed in the transport papers, so the managers of the "mastering of the past" anniversaries list their priorities: an address to the displaced persons, a wreath laid at a KZ monument . . . The public commemoration is the message for the conscience of the world. The "good old boys" around the nightly pub table know better . . .

These notes are far from an exercise in decreed mourning, but neither are they a straightforward attempt to interpret the confrontation between Dagmar Ostermann and Hans Wilhelm Münch. They are, rather, reflections, deliberations, ideas that seemed to have germinated during the lengthy shooting period of the film *Die unheimliche Begegnung-Judenstern und Hakenkreuz* [The strange encounter: Mogen David and Swastika], which keep spinning in my mind to this day. A further motivation for these thoughts was my film *Liebe das Leben, lebe den Tod* (1988) [Love life, live death].

151

The core of my deliberation is the relationship between victim and perpetrator, between totality and extermination, between immortalization and death. It is my hope that these notes will contribute to the realization of the historical time-space continuum in the individual and collective reality, as well as serve to make men aware of the position of the self and the other in present day society.

F A D E   I N

The slogan "Am deutschen Wesen wird die Welt genesen" [German essence will heal the world] brought the world nothing but an inferno with millions of corpses. The military defeat was implied. The "Endtime" scenario of a self-destructive will to redemption has changed our century considerably. This preordained designation of the essential Germanic nature of the German people did not disappear with the defeat of the Third Reich. It is as alive as ever.

There is nothing new in the complex reality of political interests, power, war, and their organization, merely a qualitative jump that goes on from where it stopped at the end of the war. The West always renewed itself by foreign means and foreign peoples. There has always been the export of Western civilization in exchange for the fascination of the exotic. But the exotic and the desired is, at the same time, always the rejected and fought against. This refers to the subconscious feeling of deficiency and the attempt to relieve that deficiency by acquiring the unknown. Simultaneously, it reveals the dread fear of this enterprise, because fear is the mirror-image principal of appropriation when such appropriation is prescribed by a collective and becomes the watchword, the battle cry, the command of the policy.

Let us turn to the scene of the crime: Auschwitz. This place symbolizes many of the industrially managed establishments that bore the designation "Concentration camp." With regard to logistics and management, these extermination enterprises were an integral part of the war industry and the belligerent society. The organizational, legal, and political seizure of the "enemy within," whether racially or politically designated, was total. It reached into the farthest corners of everyday life. The enemy was everywhere, his definition global. Within the designation "enemy," all inconsistencies were synthesized: Capital and world Jewry on one hand, world Jewry and Bolshevism on the other. How strong the lure of the foreign—or the declared foreign—must have been to release this incredible potential of destructive determination.

While the "actual" war took continuous turns for the worse, and procurement of weapons, supplies, and troop transports could hardly be managed, the genocide project was given preference. Rail transports of troops and weapons from and to Greece were canceled in favor of deportation trains carrying Jews to Auschwitz. They even used planes to deport Jewish women from North Africa to Auschwitz . . . The administration of the extermination was precise to the point of being fussy. The rail transports, called "rolling stock" in the Nazi administrative jargon, were a precise monetary operation. The SS high command entered into special agreements with the Reichsbahn for the deportations and paid them out of the stolen moneys of the Jews. With the same kind of precision, the proceeds of the utilization of the deportees would be calculated, regardless of whether it was a corpse or a still usable person. Business was extremely profitable.

The industrial establishment Auschwitz and the other concentration camps, their satellite camps, and other installations were spread out over the entire Reich area. They were given a multitude of tasks, from the physical extermination and the the converting of the corpses to industrial products such as soap, to the leasing of manpower to war industries like the Buna works [synthetic rubber production], which had its factories close to the camp area of Auschwitz.

Large transfer activities took place during the procurement of the slave labor force. All essential branches of the war industry as well as all renowned companies in the fields of chemistry, steel processing, etc., were involved in the process. The RSHA, the leading authority in the SS, representing practically a state within a state, coordinated the extermination activities. The RSHA had its own central economic office, which administered the above mentioned products of the Final Solution with precise accounting methods. This process could only succeed by tight cooperation between the SS and all other leading authorities of the Third Reich.

The death dealing, systematic functioning of the extermination machinery was neither the work of vulgar ruffians nor of perverse individuals. The desk perpetrators of national socialism pursued their strategic targets, rather, with the tools of diplomacy, with goal-oriented zeal and dutiful observance of all the laws.

Thus the bureaucracy of the "Reich" respected the sovereignty of their allies and the population of such allied countries. During the relentless "purging" of Roumania's Jewish inhabitants these people had to be "released" for deportation by a special administrative gesture. For this purpose, the trains would be stopped in the no-man's land between the Roumanian and Hungarian borders. At this point, the people in the trains were deprived of their Roumanian citizenship by officials of the Roumanian foreign office. Only by this act was the extermination, in the view of the Nazis, legally sanctioned by international law.

Here is another insight into the world of the national socialist system. After the "Crystal night" in November 1938, that in Vienna led to "spontaneous" plundering, mistreatments, killings, etc., some of the victims reported the perpetrators to the police. The police followed through on some of them, and some of the perpetrators had to pay fines. But while waiting for the results of their complaints, the plaintiffs were sent to the extermination camp, and the secured fines were sent after them to the camp. Most of the time, "because of death of the recipient," the money was not delivered. . . . In the ghetto Theresienstadt, there existed a "perfect" public assistance system and a banking system with old-age insurance.

The Nazi authorities had started an advertising campaign among the "deserving" Jews; as "deserving," they would count, perhaps, an ex-officer of the First World War, a leading medical authority, a famous musician, etc. In the campaign literature they were offered a sojourn in a spa, which turned out to be a journey to their death. In the ghetto Theresienstadt, vouchers for clothing and food were issued from the Nazi-established banking system for Nazi established Theresienstadt currency. If someone, for instance, needed socks he had to suffer through months of procedure to find the right distribution place for the vouchers. When he finally found it, there were no more socks.

Humiliation and destruction of self-confidence, exposure to cruel pro-cedures of psychic destruction were all part and parcel of the methodical extermination. Systematically degrading the victims left them helplessly open to the unlimited power of their guards and administrators.

The extermination program, called "The Final Solution," was executed with proper, bureaucratic efficiency. To this day there are many who will sentimentally and neurotically elevate these actions to heroic deeds, which, though appalling, nevertheless represented the imperative per-formance of their duty. The admixture of a cold-blooded readiness to act, male complicity, and self-pity are inherent in the destructive char-acter of the Nazi origin. After all, aren't the victims the ones to be blamed for their own culpability? Genocide and mass torture are with cynical perversion turned into a question of the victims: "How can we make amends for the fact that we inflicted Auschwitz upon the poor Germans?"

The scenario of the Third Reich borrowed various set pieces out of the prop-box of Western European retrograde utopias and paired them up with a technologically designed future. The basis for the missionary power system of the Third Reich was an all-encompassing promise of dominion and redemption, the most all-inclusive promise ever of this century in Europe. The use of human beings as building blocks of a movable pa-rade-architecture, to be used in a cinematic monumental mis-en-scène; the public ceremonial spectacle of the leader and his vassals; the specific enhancement of daily life with the help of emblems, labels, and uni-forms; the rape of the language; the repetitive slogans; the functionary titles, ranks, and authorities blended the gigantic amorphous collective into a unit that was to affirm the feeling of security, protection, and a higher destiny—a world of both challenge and relief at the same time. Relief, because the individual became a part of the whole that took re-sponsibility for him and carried him; challenge, because the individual could make himself believe that he was needed and wanted by the whole. The feeling of being needed was affirmed for the individual by a system that was dependent on his or her willing complicity. The individual man or woman became significant because the totality was significant. He or she could hide behind father and mother figures, whose existence he or she could destroy at the same time; orderly aggression is possible and deliberate. The productions of the Third Reich stylized birth and death on an apocalyptic scale.

HOW PERPETRATORS TURN INTO VICTIMS

It is strikingly peculiar how the perpetrators, in their self-evaluations see themselves transformed into victims. Hans Wilhelm Münch, who, like Rudolf Höss, the long-term commandant of Auschwitz, admits the existence of the extermination industry of Auschwitz, projects his own suffering onto the victims. He has great difficulties describing his personal experiences in Auschwitz. His sorrow, as he now states it, is caused by the victims not being able to understand his reluctance. This mechanism of "transferral" is covered under the overarching mantle of "performance of duty." He does not choose to remember the unlimited power of the SS officer in the complex called Auschwitz, not his own responsibility and his participation. What he chooses to remember is his personal fate, which was (supposedly) forced upon him.

Rudolf Höss, in his autobiographical notes, also talks in detail about the extermination system and the different behavior patterns of diverse "racial" groups among the prisoners. He is highly upset about the sadism of the SS women who beat French Jewesses to death. But he does not waste one thought on the fact that he never thought to use his power to punish the SS women nor does he acknowledge the fact that these atrocities were part of the Auschwitz system. Thus the perpetrator in the extermination process becomes the dutiful victim of history.

The rubble of history and thought frequently superimpose themselves through repression on the common mechanism in which the perpetrator-victim structure becomes manifest. One dimension of the repression of these structures becomes visible in the well-known, formulaic language of "overcoming of the past."

I previously mentioned the unique connection of a process of doubling. The genocide, the industrial extermination, the regulations, the hierarchies, and the total expediency of the system of installation as well

as the architecture of the "extermination camps" represent the culmina-
tion of the labor-intensive, organized "mass murder." The analysis of
these extermination complexes, of the organizational patterns in the
"delivery of human materials," the exploitation of labor and of bodies
points us to radical realizations, in view of such radical machinery. These
mechanisms have the potential once again to rule Austrians' daily reality.
They can be recalled and repeated in ever-changing forms. They fill language, awareness, and the media reality, their illusory product, as well as
"real" life.

Let us return to repression and its formulas, to the bureaucratically
imprinted "warehousing" of experiences. The cult that has grown around
the "overcoming the past" slogans usually wears the mask of horror and
dismay. However, the rituals suppress what they pretend to name. They
do not originate out of an insight into reality and feasibility but out of the
need to handle both, so that they can be removed from personal lives
and history and surrendered to the historic remnants of time. The individual is exonerated. Any reflective thought process dealing with the
tragedy is rejected, because it would mean recognizing that we are involved in a historical world, wherein we play an active part. We speak
about the political and social preconditions of Hitler's usurpation of power,
about the conditions that allowed the creation of the "Third Reich." We
personalize the historic events and project them into the leader- figure of
Hitler. Not one word about his empowerment. Not a word about the
societal energy, the bureaucratic fanaticism, the multibranched "self-con-
trol" upon which this power apparatus was based. The projection of a
"charismatic leader figure" is a simplified explanation formula that re-
lieves the public of having to deal with the deadly and complex reality.
Simultaneously, we see a recurrence of sly sympathy from the submis-
sive ego for the aura of domination, of the rituals and aesthetics connected with it, for the "I-negating" submersion in the group.

The current refusal to deal with questions central to the Holocaust and
national socialism, the aversion/fear to confront these facts, has its coun-
terpart in the permanent actuality of the topic. Soldier novels, highly
approved observances of cherished traditions, the war memorials throughout Austria with the inscription "Died for home and fatherland 1939–

1945," demonstrate clearly how repression and realization blend into one abysmal synthesis. This shallow cult of commemoration does not permit a consequent pursuit of the country's history; this can only occur in residues, in academic backwaters, and far away from realities that determine the day-to-day policies. To write the history of the second Austrian Republic from this point of view would probably fill a second book.

Incapable of comprehending acceptance or painful correction, the denied and repressed facts become a power that sneaks in through the backdoor. The accumulated potential of emotions and irrationalities holds sway over the world of ideas, the social structure, the societal debate. Enlightenment in its original meaning as "emancipating power of society," is resisted as a threat. In such a climate, even honest efforts of "political education" become deformed. What remains is a ritual of hopelessness, of political impotence and embittered monomania.

THE SYSTEMATIC OF EXTERMINATION

The extermination camp was arranged on strict hierarchical lines and the perpetrator elite, the SS, carefully organized the management hierarchy among the victims. At the very bottom of the ladder there was the lowly Stubenälteste. He had the responsibility for the behavior of a group of inmates while their working power was being exploited: he was responsible for their discipline, took charge of the minimal rations distribution, and had limited powers of punishment. He shared a miniscule bit of the perpetrators' splendor, had some jurisdiction over the inmates, and also some privileges. The central supply service and the kitchen were manned by KZ prisoners as well. In the fight for every ounce of bread during the distribution of the rations, internal competitions arose, which of course stimulated the black market. This hierarchical structure assured the smooth administration and extermination of the victims. The least necessary amount of calories had been precisely calculated, malnutrition sooner or later engendered death of the victims.

The Kapos were the quasi-midlevel executives, though they were also inmates. They helped with the selections, controlled the barracks, were responsible for the requisition of all properties brought into the camp by the deportees, administered the clothing warehouse, and other industrially valuable "waste material." In other areas, the SS also systematized the brief time of survival. Within the extermination machinery, the "death commando" had the task to pull the dead out of the gas chambers piece by piece and burn them in the crematories. If the crematories were overloaded, pyres were built to burn the corpses. In case of excessive overload in the gas chambers, babies and children were thrown alive on the pyres. The death commando, consisting exclusively of inmates, enjoyed a considerable amount of privileges regarding clothes and nutrition. They even received alcohol rations. But the members of the death commando had only a limited time to live. After a few months of working, each death commando was rotated directly into the gas. The commando members were aware of that. But in the Auschwitz system, any brief advantage was counted a boon in view of the daily death rate.

THE VICTIMS: RESISTANCE AND ACCEPTANCE

To be a victim meant to be subject to the stigma of finality. Facing this finality, all moments of silence, the necessity to deal with it, and the mourning centered around it are at the deepest level left to the victims. It is ludicrous to expect mourning from the perpetrators. Mourning takes place where there has been and will be great pain. In the perpetrators' view, the victims are repulsive. They are fatiguing; they generate resistance and annoyance. It is much more comfortable to be a perpetrator and to cover the psychological self-mutilation with the varnish of power.

Martin Buber, in his work *I and Thou* described the possibility of restoring a human being through the mutual respect for the other, the alien. The other and the alien are simultaneously one's own self, the so-called better half: Nothing in this dialogue is final, nothing is settled; there are no autocratic pretenses, no absolute principles. It represents the exchange between mortals, a recognition of their temporal state of existence, of the language of the soul and its longings. Among the poorest of poor, the water-carrier, the fool and the lame, you will find the face of God, who is of this world. He is the never-fixed icon of humanity on the way to the self . . . The chassidic tales, the legends of the " Thirteen Just Men," tell us of this journey.

For a national mission, for claims to world domination and extermination scenarios, one finds hardly anything useful in these legends. But just that is the threatening fact, because these tales reveal a different face of man and the world. No wonder, then, that such traditions and their bearers were stigmatized as enemies of the state. In the world of extermination, the suffering of the other is personal satisfaction and enjoyment—it needs no other existential effort. Only in the world of potential and real guilt, the phrases of "time heals all wounds" and "one forgets" are bandied about. With phrases such as these, the perpetrators confirm the legitimacy of their deeds. And they decide how memory, self-esteem, and life history of the victims should be shaped.

FLASH BACK

As a consequence of the French Revolution, German Philosophy designed a "redeemer theory" of contradiction, which was supposed to lead to a victory of the good. During the early Romantic period, poets and philosophers described the drama of man's inner strife. They described the apocalypse in the battle between light and darkness, between magic and mystery, between passion and horror, and they showed us humanity in its search for redemption.

It is common literary practice to associate the Romantic with a condition of longing and emotion, fantasy and sad sentimentality. The so-called Romantic was actually a vehement awakening of the "German soul," a rejection of the sense of order, of the conciliatory classic period and an adventurous leap into the inner spaces of an unredeemed existence. The metaphor of the ever-seeking wanderer, as, for example, in Eichendorff's *Taugenichts* [famous romantic novel], the rejection of the sham-worlds of officialdom and their conformities appeared to be a revolt against the "German essence." But soon the world would be healed by just that German essence. Eichendorff's *History of the German Literature*, Schlegel's conversion to Catholicism, and his journalistic activities in Metternich's Vienna are the first signs of the process. The ideas and concepts of the early Romantic were gradually turned into their very antithesis: allegiance to the state, religious submission, baroque ceremonial, a vague mysticism, and the discovery of the German Middle Ages as reactionary utopia of a nationalistic sense of mission became the ingredients for Germany's ruthless world mission.

Within the womb of German idealism and late Romanticism grew the linking of state, nation, history, and redemptive mission, which became the blatant ideology and mythos of the "Master Race." The dissolution of the concrete, the individual in favor of communality and its sense of destiny became the accepted norm. Insubordination against this norm was declared to be deviant and interpreted as an attempt to fight against the inner sense of the world's events and their progression. The joining of state and society, state and nation, of nation and mission, formed the basis for the "Third Reich." The apocalypse was added to this admixture. We cannot overlook the projections of redemption and endtime in the music, the philosophy, or the literature of the Nineteenth Century. They in themselves encompass the positive of the redemption and the negative of the twilight of the Gods.

Another set piece of the European intellectual history is the immortalization of the female as an artless, idealized, but at the same time terrifying being. The female is the bearer of secrets, the witch, and she possesses magic powers. This "female nature" is opposed by the male reasoning, which lacks any possibility of connecting with the mysteries of life. Rapprochement of the two sexes in such a constellation is only possible by hierarchical means, any egalitarian attempt to establish a dialogue between these two worlds is doomed to fail. Never the twain shall meet. This means, of course, that the stronger of the two inevitably oppresses the so-called "weaker sex."

All the above-described tendencies contain a rejection of the self-actualization of the "I," the "Thou," and of a social structure reform. What have these facts to do with Auschwitz and the Genocide?

Every genocide needs ideological legitimation, a message of salvation. Mostly the question was not whether or not a person announced himself as an enemy of the terrorist system. The validity of the subject was not a given, but an assessment beyond subjectivity. The proof of Aryan descent is typical for this method. It determines whether a human being is worth living or deserves to be exterminated. Man becomes the plaything of alien powers, an object of unavoidable constellations. The determination, "what is female, what is male, what is race, who is allowed to live, who must die," denies every reflexive view of what is . . . and what was. The fixation of fateful laws of life prevent everything that might represent the diversity of life. Noses, ears, skull formation, eye position, hair color, shape of feet, female pelvic structure, and breasts were measured and ranged into "racial " norms, and the inferior was exhibited with the help of live examples. The ideal man, the ideal woman, were "published" in films and photographs and presented with their family tree—as models for a segment of the population whose racial awareness could be confirmed by the Aryan certificate. Legions of scientists were entrusted with the new body construction and with the cleansing and purification of all branches of science—from physics to philosophy. A gigantic, scientific, executive body worked theoretically and concretely for the scientific proof of the superiority of the "master race." The lie of this axiom of truth was monstrous but nevertheless effective: there was not a trace of collective grumbling.

VICTIMS, PERPETRATORS, AND (THEIR) IMMORTALIZATION

Let us observe the "deed" from a realistic aspect. In their solid existence, facts determine the foundations of our reality. For example, a woman looses a breast to cancer, an accident leads to the amputation of a leg, etc., Such facts have the character of finality, and they approach the absolute finality, death. No manner of solace, be it religion or any other form of belief, can cancel the fact; it only helps to learn to deal with it. The power of the factual demands intensive pursuit. It runs the gamut from shock, repression, and search for meaning to redemption theories. Even the "coming to terms with something" is an attempt to find consolation and redemption.

While the act of destruction confronts us with finality, the mirror-image world of human restoration is always at risk. The soft, the fragile, love, affection, and the world of vulnerable emotions show us a sensitive cosmos threatened by destruction. This cosmos is not infinite, it can be destroyed at a moment's notice. The magical circles of "good" and "evil" represent this original dilemma in all human dramas. The key point in this drama is again a fact. A deed, once done, cannot be recalled, cannot be erased.

The more decisive and powerful an impact the deed has on the facts, the more vehement the preoccupation with it—if only to repress it. We, therefore, live in a split situation in which we are simultaneously victim and perpetrator—and this subjective drama of collective dissemination turns, as is the case with Auschwitz, into evil magic. Such magic is commonplace, it is routine. Because of that it has extraordinary efficacy. It intensifies the accepted, the self-evident, the defeat of the other as precondition for one's own power and victory.

When we speak of the "beyond" within us or are motivated to act by this dilemma, it also clearly implies a relation to the temporal. Therefore, I propose the thesis that every act of extermination—that is to say, every form of killing—is an attempt for immortalization of the self, a blacking-out of mortality. He who destroys puts himself outside of the temporal— and therein the contradiction is already apparent. One destroys in order to immortalize one self and with this act confirms, simultaneously, the impossibility of escaping temporal existence.

The acceptance of the finiteness of life creates goodness, understanding, and tranquillity. This process is the topic of the particular literature that flamed on book-burning pyres of the Nazis. Denying the temporality of our existence through master race, world redemption, and apocalyptic finale creates death, the final fact of time. The dialectic of self-preservation and killing through the illusory extinction of time becomes apparent in the extermination policies of the Third Reich. The killing of death is performed as the liberation from mortality. This liberation, in turn, creates death. The extinction of time—as the dimension between birth and death—establishes the rule of time in all its power. The killing of the alien lives (as the deadly enemy . . . as capitalistic-bolshevistic Jewish world conspiracy) is brought into the world as the instrument of self-immortalization of the "Third Reich." Consequently, the mythology of the Third Reich lies not only in the production of the extermination of the alien, but also in the compulsive-neurotic production of its own temporal apocalypse.

The words "purification" and "cleansing" were common usage in the everyday life of the NS regime. Cleansing and purification are protective measures: hygiene prescribes it. It is easy to imagine how compulsive such collective practices are and how firmly they are embedded in a neurotic lifestyle. The "Cleansing" is such an immense task that every step of it must be executed so carefully and precisely that the dirt has time enough to accumulate again right behind it. This is not only the dilemma of the "housewife." The cleansing tasks in the "Third Reich" were so immense that they confronted the executors—in spite of all efforts—over and over again with filth. One thing above all never succeeded: the liquidation of the liquidation center: Auschwitz (in spite of blowing up the gaschambers and exhuming the corpses). The cleansing left its own filth behind. Ergo, the murder of death, the attempted destruction of time by killing an apocalyptic enemy-construct (the quintessential death threat for the master race), only creates death anew and thereby confirms the victory of the inevitable facts of time and the finiteness of life.

In view of permanent wars and deaths, this thought process appears absurd, but it is confirmed through them. Death as a reality and a metaphor must be advanced all the more radically the more it is being denied. A backdoor of this contradiction remains open through the thesis of the collective salvation. Every death assures the immortality of a race destined to rule and assures its worldwide, historic mission. The lie is, generally speaking, a matter of morals. However, in the totalitarian system the lie is the offspring of truth. Where there is no irony, there is no distance; where there is no distance, there is no reflecting perception. If there is no reflection, there is no self in learning and development; where there is no learning and development, there is no laughter but only death fixation. The totalitarian truth opposes, destroys, and extinguishes what it claims to mean. In its dictatorial mission, it has plowed through all areas of life and cleansed them from "filth." Literature, music, dance, food, clothing, film, down to the most everyday existence were permeated by that one valid truth. Even the chess game was "aryanized." Many of the chess masters were Jews. The Jewish chess player was turned into an unimaginative, desiccated opponent who opened every game with a devious move. An Aryan, upright, and combative opening move was developed against him. This tactic became not only the ideology for every club, but also the self-evident exercise in national socialist virility and the main virtue of the "Volksgemeinschaft" [tr. note: a term that had meaning far beyond the word "community." It contained the implication of Aryan and Germanic exclusivity].

Auschwitz was neither an "Industrial Accident" nor an enclave of perversion; it is inscribed in the German intellectual and social history. Many genocides occurred under the banner of missionary world redemption—from the conquest of Byzantium under the sign of the cross to the extermination of the North American natives to the subjugation of the blacks, etc. However, Auschwitz as an industrial extermination enterprise of highest perfection, was indisputably the high point of organized management of murder. Auschwitz was the logical consequence of a history of Western extermination policies, which aimed at eliminating the remaining antagonists in their own middle.

Appendixes
Glossary
Index

Appendix A

BIOGRAPHICAL DATA

DAGMAR OSTERMANN (née Bock) was born in Vienna in 1920. Her father, born in Vienna, was a Jew. Her German mother was a Baptist. The parents divorced in 1924. The mother married a Jewish attorney, who died in 1931. Dagmar Ostermann spent her childhood and adolescence in Vienna, but she frequently visited her grandmother in Dresden. She quit an apprenticeship in an office and visited a business school owned by Jews, which was immediately closed after the Anschluss [March 13, 1938, German annexation of Austria]. One of her uncles, who came to Vienna with the occupiers and stayed at his sister's apartment, took her illegally to Dresden where she worked in a clothing factory until 1940.

In August 1942, she was summoned by the Gestapo because of alleged illegal contacts with "Aryans" and was kept in the Dresden Gestapo prison. In September 1942, she was sent via Berlin to the concentration camp Ravensbrück and from there, in October 1942, to Auschwitz. There she worked in the Political Section [registry] until April 1944. She was sent to the penal commando and from there to Ravensbrück once more.

On May 2, 1945, she was liberated near the town of Mecklenburg by American troops. She made her way (for the better part on foot) to Vienna where she arrived on May 31, 1945. In 1947 she married Fred Ostermann, a Jewish refugee, who spent the war with the partisans in Yugoslavia; a son, Frank, was born of this marriage.

The couple opened a successful fashion business. Divorced in 1964, Dagmar Ostermann ran a newspaper-and-tobacco kiosk until her retirement. For the last twelve years she has been—and still is—very active as an invaluable witness and lecturer on the Holocaust in Austrian schools. She has been honored by the city of Vienna as well as by the Federal Austrian government for her untiring efforts on behalf of the Holocaust and its victims

DR. HANS WILHELM MÜNCH was born in 1911 in Freiburg/Breisgau. He spent his childhood in the country, where his father was a forest superintendent. He visited the gymnasium [secondary school] in Dresden. He studied medicine from 1933–35 in Tübingen and, from 1935–38, in Munich. During the summer of 1935 he joined the national socialist motorcycle brigade (NSKK); in September 1937, he joined the party. During his studies (completed in 1938) he authored a scientific study about living conditions in the Bayerische Wald [a region of southern Germany]. He obtained a scholarship to work at the Institute of Hygiene in Munich from 1936–38; from 1937–1939, he worked at the Schwabinger Krankenhaus [hospital in Munich]. He married a fellow student, and together with her, assumed "emergency duties" for country physicians who had been drafted into the military. He worked from fall 1939 until 1940 in Steingaden and until 1943 in Lechbruck. He has two children, born 1940 and 1942. In June 1943 he joined the Waffen SS [the fighting branch of the SS], followed by a brief military and medical officer training in Stettin and Graz. From January 1944 until January 1945, he was active at the Institute of Hygiene in Auschwitz, working in the area of epidemics prevention. From March 1945 to May 1945, he was in Dachau, setting up a bacteriological institute. In summer 1945 he reported to an American POW camp near Stuttgart. After approximately two months, he was identified as an SS officer and was sent to a special camp [Kornwestheim Barracks], and from there he was extradited to a prison in Poland [First at Dachau, March to summer 1946 in Breslau, and from 1946 to 1948 in Krakau]. He was acquitted in 1947 [see appendix B]. He was active as a country doctor from 1948 until his retirement in 1990.

Appendix B

EXCERPT FROM THE ACQUITTAL OF DR. HANS
WILHELM MÜNCH IN THE PROCEEDINGS AGAINST
LIEBEHENSCHEL ET AL.

Notarized Translation from the Polish, Frankfurt/Main, June 3, 1961

The highest people's tribunal acquitted the accused 8) Hans Wilhelm
Münch of all accusations for the reason that the accused, as is apparent
from the findings in part III, not only did not commit any crimes detri-
mental to the camp inmates but, on the contrary, was favorably inclined
towards them and, in a manner that could entail severe penalties for him,
helped them without any consideration of race, religion, or political convictions. He also sabotaged the rules of the German camp authorities,
and, aside from being a member of the SS, where he was forcibly in-
ducted, Münch did not belong to any national socialist organization. In
these circumstances it will have to be assumed that the accused Münch
has not been ideologically connected either with the organization of the
SS, the members of the authorities, the administration and the garrison
of the Auschwitz camp, or with the Institute of Hygiene in Rajsk, where
he was active as physician and bacteriologist. The accused did not take
part in any of the criminal associations, and, therefore, he must be acquitted according to the principles of the Nurnberg judgment. (Thesis 19)

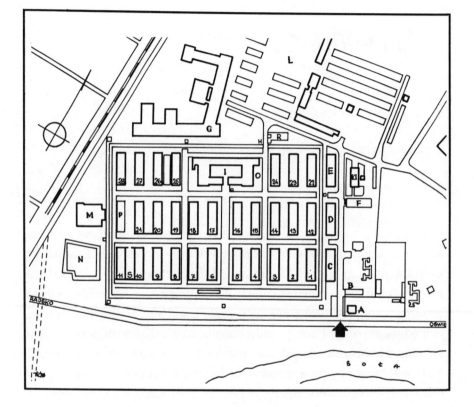

Appendix C

MAPS OF AUSCHWITZ AND ITS RAIL LINES

AUSCHWITZ I (Opposite)

A   Camp Commander's residence

B   Main guard station

C   Commander's office building

D   Camp administration

E   SS hospital

F   Office of the Political Section (Camp Gestapo)

G   Admissions

H   Gate with inscription *Arbeit macht frei*

I   Kitchen

KI   Gaschamber and crematorium I

L   Farm buildings and workshops

M   Warehouses for belongings taken from the dead (gassed prisoners)

N   Gravel pit (execution place)

O   Place where camp orchestra used to play

P   Laundry barracks for SS

R   SS blockleader building

S   Execution wall

1-28 Prisoner housing

Source: Interpress Warszawa/Tadeusz Kinowski

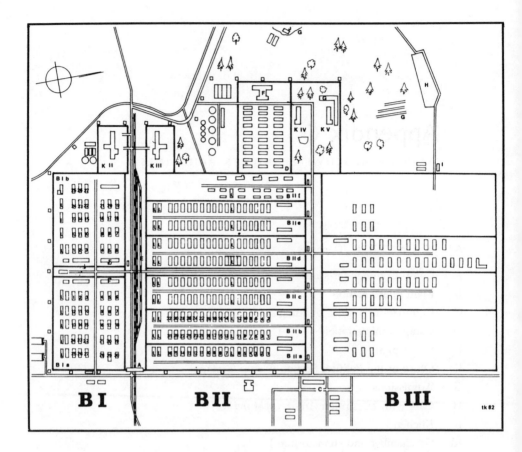

AUSCHWITZ II—BIRKENAU (Opposite)

Sections

A   Main guard station with tower

BI   First camp section

BII   Second camp section

BIII   Third camp section, under construction (Mexico)

BIa   Women's camp

BIb   Projected men's camp for 1943, to be added to women's camp

BIIa   Quarantine camp

BIIb   Theresienstadt Jewish family camp

BIIc   Hungarian Jewish camp

BIId   Men's camp

BIIe   Gypsy camp

BIIf   Prisoners' camp infirmary

C   SS headquarters and barracks

D   Warehouses for goods robbed from the victims

E   Arrival ramp where transports were unloaded and selections performed

F   Saunas

G   Pyres for burning corpses when ovens broke down

H   Mass graves of Russian POWs

I   First temporary gaschamber

J   Second temporary gaschamber

KII   Gaschamber and crematorium II

KIII   Gaschamber and crematorium III

KIV   Gaschamber and crematorium IV

KV   Gaschamber and crematorium V

L   Latrines and washbarracks

Prisoner barracks have arabic numbers.
Section BIII was under construction when Auschwitz was evacuated.

Source: Interpress Warszawa/Tadeusz Kinowski

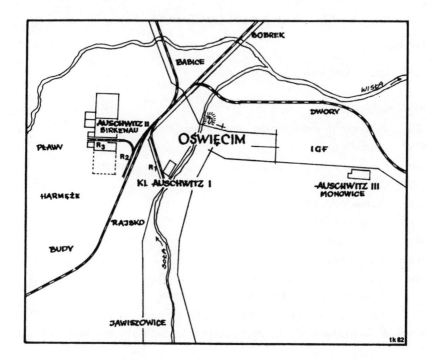

THE RAIL SIDINGS CONNECTING AUSCHWITZ I, I I, AND III CAMPS

R_1 Siding from main rail line to Auschwitz I

R_2 Siding for unloading Jewish transports
         ("The Jew Ramp")

R_3 Siding in Auschwitz II to crematoriums

IGF   Building site of IG-Farben's chemical
         installation (Buna-Monowitz, synthetic rubber
         manufacture)

The Institute for Hygiene was located in Rajsko.

Source: Interpress Warzawa/Tadeusz Kinowski

Appendix D

RANK COMPARISONS OF THE WAFFEN-SS
AND GERMAN ARMY

Waffen-SS Rank	*Army Rank*
SS-Obergruppenführer	General
SS-Obersturmbannführer	Lt. Colonel
SS-Sturmbannführer	Major
SS-Hauptsturmführer	Captain
SS-Obersturmführer	lst Lieutenant
SS-Untersturmführer	Second Lieutenant

Non-Commissioned Officers	
SS-Hauptscharführer	First Sergeant
SS-Oberscharführer	Sergeant
SS-Unterscharführer	N.C.O.

Other Ranks	
SS-Rottenführer	Lance-corporal
SS-Sturmmann	Pfc
SS-Mann	Private

Appendix E

Amery, Jean (1912–1978) a.k.a. Hans Mayer. Austrian author, committed suicide in 1978.

Auerbach, Philipp. Former Auschwitz prisoner. After 1945, head of Prisoner Reparations Office, Munich.

Bock, Oswald. Father of Dagmar Ostermann (née Bock). Died March 8, 1944, in Auschwitz-Birkenau gas chamber.

Böck, Richard. Ambulance driver in Birkenau, refused transporting Zyklon-B and was transferred to Russian front, according to Hermann Langbein.

Boger, Wilhelm. SS-Oberscharführer in the Political Section in Auschwitz, invented the "Boger Swing." His name is erroneously spelled "Bogner."

Broad, Perry. SS-Rottenführer from 1942 on. Active in the Political Section. Conducted interrogations and was responsible for providing the Auschwitz I brothel with women.

Caesar, Dr. Joachim. SS-Obersturmbannführer, Head of the Agriculture Section in Auschwitz.

Celan, Paul (1920–1970) a.k.a. Paul Anczel. Jewish-Austrian lyrical poet. Committed suicide.

Clauberg, Prof. Carl. Gynecologist. Head of the Medical Experiments Institute in Auschwitz.

Delmotte, Dr. Hans. SS-Untersturmführer. Physician at The Hygiene Institute, Auschwitz. Committed suicide in 1945.

Dürrmayer, Dr. Heinrich. Prisoner camp elder (highest position for prisoner) in Auschwitz. According to H. Langbein, he worked with the resistance ("fighting group Auschwitz").

Erber, a.k.a. Hustek. SS-Unterscharführer. Worked in Political Section, Auschwitz.

Grabner, Maximilian. SS-Untersturmführer. Director of Political Section, Auschwitz, 1942–1944.

Hasse, Elisabeth. Chief SS-Matronin Budy, Agriculture Sector.

Hecht. Prisoner in Dr. Münch's Hygiene Institute Commando.

Heydrich, Reinhard, (1904–1942). SS-Obergruppenführer. From 1934, Head of Gestapo, Berlin; 1939, Head of Reichs Security Main Office (RSHA); from 1941, Head of overall planning for "The Final Solution of the Jewish Question." Assassinated by Czech underground in Prague, 1942.

Himmler, Heinrich (1900–1945). From 1929 Reichsführer-SS. From 1939 in charge of so-called Resettlement and Germanisation policies in Eastern and South Eastern Europe. Had jurisdiction over "Final Solution." Committed suicide in 1945.

Hitler, Adolf (1889–1945). Chancellor of the Third Reich. Committed suicide in 1945.

Höss, Rudolf (1900–1947). SS-Hauptsturmführer. First commandant of Auschwitz from May 1940–November 1943. Recalled to Auschwitz to supervise exterminations of Hungarian Jews in 1944. Executed by Polish Court, 1947.

Hössler, Franz. SS-camp leader of women's camp Auschwitz-Birkenau from August 1943–January 1945.

Kirschner, Herbert. SS-Oberscharführer. Head of Political Section, Auschwitz, 1942–1945.

Kristan, Bernhard. SS-Unterscharführer. Worked in the registry office under SS-Oberscharführer Quackernack.

Lachmann, Gerhard. SS-Unterscharführer. Interrogated prisoners in the Political Section.

Langbein, Hermann. Political prisoner transferred from KZ Dachau to Auschwitz, August 20, 1942. Well-known author of *Menschen in Auschwitz*, one of the classic documentations on Auschwitz.

Liebehenschel, Arthur. SS-Obersturmbannführer. Commandant of KZ Auschwitz from November 1943–May 1944.

Lingens-Reiner, Ella. Dr. med. Prisoner Physician. Worked with Dr. Mengele.

Mengele, Josef, Dr. med. (1911–1979). Geneticist. Performed numerous pseudoscientific experiments on twins in Auschwitz-Birkenau.

Moll, Otto. SS-Hauptscharführer. Specialist for disposal of corpses. Head of the Auschwitz-Birkenau crematoriums from 1943–1944, then camp commandant of satellite camp Gleiwitz.

Mrugowski, Joachim, Prof. med. Head of the SS Hygiene Institute, Berlin.

Oppenheimer, Leo. Jewish schoolfriend of Dr. Münch in Munich.

Pohlhas. Chief Inspector of Gestapo, Dresden.

Pyschny, Heinrich. SS-Sturmmann. Worked as a guard in the Political Section. Took part in selection at ramp and in gassings. He tried to help prisoners and was frequently arrested. After the war he was acquitted by a Polish court.

Rosenberg, Alfred (1893–1946). Journalist and politician. Leading theoretician of the SS ideology; from 1923 publisher of the *Völkische Beobachter*, the National Socialist Party organ; established Research Institute for the Jewish question and in his position as head of the institute, confiscated art objects and valuables confiscated from Jews in all occupied countries. Convicted and hung in Nuremberg.

Schmidt, Otto. SS-Unterscharführer. Worked in the Political Section.

Schumann, Horst, Dr. med. Specialist in x-ray sterilization from 1942–44 in Auschwitz. Dr. Münch quotes him mistakenly as Schuhmacher.

Schurz, Hans. SS-Untersturmführer. From May 1943, attached to Political Section. Became head of Political Section in November 1943.

Schuschnigg, Kurt von (1897–1977). Austrian chancellor, 1934–1938.

Stark, Hans. SS-Oberscharführer. Worked in admissions office of Auschwitz (main camp) since 1941.

Strassburger, Julius. Dubious personality supposedly working at the Hygiene Institute, Munich, and on Heydrich's staff.

Streicher, Julius (1885–1946). Founded the yellow-press newspaper *Der Stürmer*, in 1923. Convicted and hung in Nuremberg, 1946.

Waldheim, Kurt. Austrian politician. Was Austrian secretary of state as well as secretary general of the UN. In spite of the revelations of his national socialist past, he was elected president of Austria.

Weber, Bruno. SS-Obersturmführer. Head of the Hygiene Institute in Auschwitz. Also head physician of Auschwitz-Birkenau from 1942–1944.

Zimmetbaum, Mala (1918–1944). Belgian Jewish prisoner, who fled with her friend, Edward Galinski, on June 24, 1944. Recaptured, tortured, and murdered on July 6, 1944.

Glossary

Arbeitsdienst: department responsible for assigning the prisoners to various work details.

Arbeitsdienstführer/in: SS-labor control officer who supervised Arbeitsdienst.

Arbeitskommando: work detail.

Aufseherin: female SS overseer, also translated as "matron."

Aussenkommando: external work detail (field work, road building, railroad building, etc.) within camp perimeter and surrounding areas.

BDM: Bund Deutscher Mädchen, female equivalent of Hitler Youth.

Blockälteste (Blockova, Polish form): prisoner in charge of a block (barrack)

Blockführer/in: SS man or matron responsible for a block.

Blockschreiber/in: recording secretary and assistant to the Blockälteste.

Bunker: cellblock in the basement of block 11 of Auschwitz I used for severe punishment and torture of prisoners.

Erzgebirge: mountain range on German-Czech border.

Kanada: name for the small camp in Auschwitz-Birkenau, where the personal belongings of victims were sorted, stored, and sent into the Reich to clothes the civilian population.

Kapo: male and/or female inmate who was in charge of a labor commando or an administrative commando. A considerable number of male and female Kapos were professional criminals.

Kommandoführer/in: SS personnel in charge of an Aussenkommando.

Krankenbau: the so-called camp infirmaries at Auschwitz and Auschwitz-Birkenau. Location of frequent selections in Auschwitz-Birkenau.

Krukenkreuz: symbol of Austrian ruling party until 1938.

KZ: commonly used abreviation for "Konzentrationslager"-Concentration camp.

Lagerältester: senior administrative prisoner of a camp.

Lagerführer: highest SS officer in a camp, responsible to the Lagerkommandant (Hössler was Lagerführer of Birkenau).

Lagerkommandant: the commandant of an entire concentration or death camp. Responsible directly to Himmler. (Höss was "Lagerkommandant" of the whole Auschwitz Complex).

Muselmann, Muselmänner: Auschwitz jargon for male or female prisoners who through hunger and disease have been so weakened that they have become the daily fodder for the selections to the gas.

NS: Nationalsozialist [National Socialist]. All Nazi organizational abbreviations started with *NS*.

NSKK: National Sozialistisches Kraftfahrzeug Kommando-Motorcycle unit of the Nazi organization.

Oberaufseherin: headmatron in Auschwitz-Birkenau, female equivalent of Lagerführer.

organize: concentration camp jargon for stealing or scrounging, clothing, food, etc., that frequently made the difference between life and death. If caught, prisoners were put into penal commando or, in severe cases, executed.

Politische Abteilung: the Political Section representing, in Auschwitz-Birkenau, the Gestapo. Maintained the registry of arrival, life, and death of all inmates, watched over prisoner "crimes" such as unauthorized contact between inmates, with civilians, or with SS. Birkenau had its own Political Section. Ostermann worked in the Politische Abteilung in Auschwitz, the main section.

Rapportführer/in: SS-in charge of roll calls within his/her assigned area

Rassenschande: strict prohibition of sexual relations between Aryans and Jews, according to the Nueremberg racial laws.

RSHA, a.k.a Reichssicherheitshauptamt: the organization under Adolf Eichmann with the designation IV B4, which was in charge of all security questions and the Final Solution.

SA: Sturm Abteilung. These were the original "Hitler's Brownshirts."

SS: Schutzstaffel, name for unit that was Hitler's elite guard. It literally means "protection detachment." Hitler elevated them to the status of sacred cadre of noble Nazi defenders. As "Waffen-SS" they became a part of the fighting force as well as the organization in charge of all concentration and extermination camps.

Selection: a very innocuous word that, in the concentrationary universe, took on the meaning of the decision between life and death. SS doctors, or sometimes even administrators, would select those they considered unfit for work to be sent to the gas.

Sonderkommando: the commando of Jewish inmates chosen to take the corpses out of the gas chamber, strip them of all valuables, and expedite them to the ovens. They would be periodically rotated into the gas themselves because they knew too much of the extermination process.

Stabsgebäude: main administrative building in Auschwitz I. Secretaries were quartered in the basement of the building.

Strafkommando: penal commando.

Stubova: lowest ranking member of the prisoner administrative staff in a block.

Stürmer, Der: Jew-baiting German newspaper under direction of Julius Streicher.

Völkische Beobachter, Der: official Newspaper of the National Socialist Party in Germany.

Waffen-SS Hygiene Institut: the medical and research facility in Auschwitz that was responsible for the control of epidemic diseases to protect the health of the SS-personnel.

Zählappell: roll call taking place in Auschwitz and Auschwitz-Birkenau every morning before marching out to work and every evening after the commandoes returned to the camp. Every inmate, male or female, would be counted twice daily. Sometimes selections were combined with the roll call.

Index